the
search
for
11:11

the
search
for
11:11

by

George Mathieu Barnard

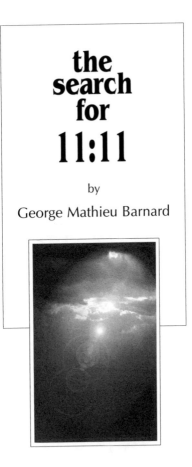

A Journey into the Spirit World

11.11
Publishers

Australia

11.11 Publishers
Australia

1111publishers.com
1111spiritguardians.com

First published on CD-ROM by 11.11 Publishers Pty Ltd, 2000

National Library of Australia Cataloging-in-Publication

Barnard, George Mathieu
    The search for 11:11 : a journey into the spirit
world / George Barnard.— 2nd ed.

    ISBN 0 9577889 6 7

    1. Guardian angels. 2. Guides (Spiritualism).

    I. Title.

    (Series: 11:11 documents)

    133.9

Printed in the United States of America
10 9 8 7 6 5 4 3 2 1

To
Sandy, Carolyn, Judy, Marsha,
Heather and Alex, Bob, Jerry,
Miguel Angel, George, Henry,
Elianne, Phillip, and Byron

Your support in getting this
book to press and your
contributions to the 11:11
Progress Group and its many
activities have been invaluable.

Disclaimer

Some names and locations have been altered to protect family, friends, and patients.

Claimer

For those who like the unexpected: There is humor and sadness—an insight into the hectic life, challenges, and emotions of an industrialist-therapist-student-husband-father-psychic healer . . . all rolled into one. Experience an escape with this mortal rookie, George Mathieu Barnard, into another reality—another dimension of time—and for a time.

For those who study human behavior: Meet the "Characters."

For those who modify human behavior: Here are a number of approaches, as well as wild—and not so wild —theories about the anatomy of the human mind, spirit, and soul . . . and Time.

For those who are searching for a more spiritual life: Here is one way of doing it.

And for those who rightly call themselves illumined, relate to the Light, call themselves Urantians, are graduates of the Great Master's Golden Flame—and even those who suspect "that seagull" might not be a bird: Meet some of your distant cousins, the 1,111 Spirit Guardians of the Temporal Halfway Realm (and others) in multidimensional time, and treasure this epic journey.

CONTENTS

Celestial Foreword

"This book is the first in a series of accounts that portray the cooperation possible between those of the Temporal Midway Realm and an ordinary mortal. These individuals constitute the 11:11 Emergency Platoon as it is functioning here on Earth. The particular series of episodes of human/celestial cooperation experienced by the author of this book is extraordinary, long lasting, frequently utilized, multifaceted, and intense— and greatly rewarding. Others can also achieve this kind of contact, though perhaps to a more limited degree.

"I am Midwayer Mathew."

"Mathew," who uses that name for convenience, communicated the above statement. As is the case with his many Seraphic Superiors, the use of numbers or codes is more common than names, as the former are more speedily communicated.

Mathew's code-name is 33-333. His presence is frequently made known through time-prompts at 3:33 AM or PM precisely, in all time zones across the globe. Mathew is a Spirit Guide, a Planetary Helper who operates in what is called the Midway Realm; therefore, like his counterparts, he is often referred to as a Midwayer.

This amazing being is on long-term but temporary loan to us. Numerous Planetary Helpers, or Celestial Volunteers, are presently on loan to our mortal races for the advancement, or upstepping, of spirituality on this Earth. We are told by Mathew that he is one of a great number of volunteers and new contacts of his kind. He was sent here by special request—his request to join the 11:11 Platoon.

x

Author's Preface

Now that I am in my sixties, I can look back over a lifetime of frequent verbal and visual contact with celestial beings—the kind I describe in this book. Even from my early childhood, I could see these spirit visitors, whom I simply thought of as my family's "spirit friends," who regularly visited my home, mostly at mealtimes. But it was obvious to me that our visitors would go to their own homes to eat dinner, since there was no more room at our table. They just seemed to hang around, patiently waiting for the meal to end, as if they wanted to draw my parents aside for casual conversation.

I had no inkling that, of the eight other members in my family, not one was aware of these celestial arrivals, though it did seem strange that no one ever talked with them. And it was hardly my place to address them, for small children were meant to be seen, not heard, at the table.

All throughout my teenage years, I received countless prompts from these beings, and because of the positive advice these prompts contained, I renamed my friends the Spirit Guides. And although I saw them less often, their valuable guidance had a highly positive impact on my life—in my studies for business management and industrial psychology, in my work, and even in my decision to leave Europe to settle in Australia as a lone migrant at age eighteen. They especially helped me in new business ventures.

From the time I was twenty until I turned thirty-two, as I cared for my young family, my contact with these spirit friends was sporadic. I seldom heard their voices, and yet their subliminal input about the future was an almost daily event. I understood their input to be pure intuition on my part, and all who knew me well pictured me as a talented psychic, capable of hitting the nail on the head when it came to predicting future events.

That conception was about to change—drastically.

When my seven-year-old daughter—at the insistence of her own "spirit playmate"—saved our entire family from certain demise, it became vital for me to urgently reacquaint myself with the Spirit Guides who, in fact, had never deserted me. Overcommitted to both business and clinical work and chronically fatigued, I had utterly failed to notice their persistent 11:11 time-prompt warnings about a grave danger to our young family of five.

It took our daughter's ability to pick up the message of her unseen playmate for me to realize that I had lost contact with something that was precious to me and that I wanted back. The urgency I felt to rediscover my spirit friends prompted an intensive search to find out where these childhood acquaintances could possibly be in time and space.

I had long assumed there was a simple genetic reason for my extended family's closeness with these Spirit Guides. My mother often conversed with unseen celestial beings, and her father was widely respected for his having been "a great dowser" in his younger years.

When I finally faced the Spirit Guides myself and looked them in the eyes for the first time, a powerful bond was established, and a remarkable Celestial-Mortal Alliance evolved. I began to count on them for assistance more often, and they more frequently depended on my doing their bidding. As they led me out of danger on a number of occasions, I renamed them the 11:11 Spirit Guardians.

These new spirit friends guarded me closely, and we soon became much more involved with the welfare of those around us. We were, and still are, a Celestial-Mortal Alliance for Progress simply called the unit, or the emergency platoon.

But they were still just my old childhood friends—revisited.

As my contact with the 11:11 Spirit Guardians grew closer, my business ventures picked up even more, and on occasion we boldly took on the task of troubleshooting and breathing new life into near-bankrupt companies. My celestial friends regularly advised me about my personal life and assisted me in countless emergencies that involved many of my patients. They even helped me to design specific therapies for clients in great need.

In 1992, I promised the celestials I would begin the big task of documenting our nearly countless combined endeavors, in order to reveal to others the exciting opportunities for cooperating with these hard-working planetary helpers. They wanted as many people as possible to read about the successes that can be achieved, the wondrous healings that take place with their aid, and the fascinating revelations about our planet and life in the greater cosmos—as well as about the spiritual advancement an association with them has to offer.

Unlike us "temporary" mortals, who live on Earth for such a short span, the 11:11 Spirit Guardians are the permanent citizens of this planet. They are capable of causing—through you and me—many small and grand events for the benefit of all, today and into the planet's distant future.

If you yearn for a more rewarding, more spiritual existence, be aware of their 11:11 and other double-digit time-prompts on your clocks, VCRs, microwave ovens. The brilliantly minded 11:11 Spirit Guardians are seeking worldwide human involvement for their task of promoting planetary progress and greater spiritual awareness.

Perhaps you too will join a Celestial-Mortal Alliance for the benefit of all.

Who Are They?

They are only human, still.
Raw products of His creation and evolution—
    flesh and blood mortals—who are invited to chart
His seas of affection, His oceans of devotion,
    in their shared existence.

Briskly put upon the intricate road to perfection,
    but awaiting a warm welcome in Eternity,
    these heirs to His universes
    fit their appreciation of His great Gifts
    in but an egg cup, still.

part one

✹

The Fourth Generation

For every meal in the Barnard homestead, over a period of more than four years, an extra place was set at the dining room table. This place, directly to George's right, was for Simone. George never saw Simone eat anything. In fact, he never saw Simone. She was invisible—but not to his eldest daughter.

To the six-and-a-half-year-old, Danielle, Simone was very real. On a few occasions, the advice that was supposed to have come from Danielle's "invisible sister" made excellent sense.

"Simone suggests you eat at least half of your green beans," the father jokingly told Danielle at their Saturday evening meal.

The youngster gave him a troubled, sullen look. Then she pounded her little fork down hard on one of the offending beans.

"That one is quite dead now," George informed her. "You killed it. I think you can safely put it in your mouth now. It won't be able to get away."

Her shoulders hunched, her lips pressed tight, Danielle kept glaring at the annoying little green trespassers on her plate. She wasn't going to show him she enjoyed the humor. She simply hated those dreadful beans too much.

The father carried on softly, "When I was little—and I was always very, very little—your grandmother cooked us only one meal per week, on Sundays. And so, on all the other days we had to eat grass, like your pony does. Green beans are ever so much nicer than grass."

The child turned on him in anger and proclaimed loudly, "When you were little—and you were always very, very little—Grandpa forgot to teach you how to walk. And so you skipped around on one leg for the rest of your life. We know that story already, too!"

She was clearly advising her father on behalf of her siblings, and perhaps on behalf of the invisible little Simone, that none of them would believe he was ever forced to eat grass.

"You ask Simone about it," George suggested. "See what she's got to say. She'll soon give you the score."

"She says the tree is going to fall on the house, Daddy," came the immediate but utterly inappropriate reply. It was the second time George had heard that comment. It was no longer a joke. He was beginning to feel uneasy.

From his place at the table, he glanced at the big White Eucalypt. It stood fully forty meters from the homestead, right on their boundary fence. There was no chance of it falling on their home. It was old, big, wide, but not very tall. It did, however, carry some large dead branches.

Perhaps they should be taken down? Be made safe? he mused.

Danielle's remark still bothered him that evening, but even trying hard as he did, he could extract no further information from his Spirit Friends. And to this day, he has no idea why they either did not know, would not tell him, or could not tell him, what he wanted to know about the potential danger with that tree.

Could this failure to obtain psychic information have been caused by fatigue?

1

"Simone Says. . ."

There were many periods during which George Barnard considered himself to be psychically depleted. During times when his firm was financially overextended, or when his workload was committing him to carry on until the early morning hours, it would be more accurate to describe the psychic as intuitively dead.

This was one of those periods.

A new machine-parts manufacture and assembly project would stretch the resources of the Barnards' family company to their very limit. Many months prior to the commencement of the sizable new undertaking, George still had some doubts about signing up for it.

As it was—especially for that time of the year—a seemingly unstoppable flow of orders had kept everyone in the firm on their toes. Tempers were frayed. Along with his workers, Barnard was tired, overworked, and somewhat indecisive.

The machine parts contract would need to be signed within a few months. That huge new commitment will swiftly push the firm's bank balance into a deep pit full of red ink, he thought. Already there was a shortage of funds, although, so far, George was the only one who had missed out on his salary—for five weeks.

Jodi, George's wife of ten years, was finding it tough to make ends meet. She was making some loud noises about being an unseen but important part of his workforce, and about being entitled to receive something extra when his "boatload of outstanding money" finally came in. At least George could charge his hypnotherapy patients for his services, she suggested. Too many of them were never charged a penny if they were rather poor.

Barnard was used to juggling his time between his family, his business, and his hypnotherapy clinic, and moderately successful at serving these three masters. Even then, he still occasionally found time to work on his designs for new machines or cameras. But those drawings had been gathering dust for months. Right now there was simply not a minute to spare.

Kevin Weiss, the firm's production manager, ambled into his boss's workroom, his clenched fists firmly in the pockets of his coveralls—a sure sign of another imminent confrontation between the two men.

No prize for guessing what's on his mind, Barnard thought. Here we go again.

"We're doing far too many different things already," Weiss suggested. "George, it could break us. We're only just managing what we've got."

Barnard put down his inking pen and ruler. He looked up at the worried production man, frowning, but without saying a word.

"It's outside our area of expertise," Weiss carried on. "Our lunchroom is too small, our toilet facilities are insufficient, factory space is already at a premium, and that stupid old forklift is about to fall apart."

"We would employ five more people, Kev," Barnard suggested. "but we more than double our turnover. This is our opportunity to grow from handkerchief size—bypassing napkin size—to tablecloth size. We gain critical mass to make us infinitely more profitable, better organized, less overworked—hopefully smarter—because we will have time to think, rather than both of us just doing things. It could be a Godsend."

Weiss turned away, shrugged, and walked to the door, his hands still in his pockets. He knew it would upset his employer. "The French are stubborn," he remarked, "and the Dutch can never be convinced of anything. You're half of each and that's what makes you so damned impossible." Weiss was getting personal. "I don't know why they let people like you migrate to Australia . . . allow you into the country."

"Ah! A mongrel! Well! It could be your German ancestry that makes you so rude and bullheaded," Barnard countered, knowing neither of them quite meant what they were saying.

Without the benefit of formal managerial training on his part, the somewhat pessimistic, fearful, but obstinate Kevin Weiss often sought to influence the highly educated Barnard's more radical schemes and decisions. This time he walked out without a further word, haughty, snubbing his boss.

George's stomach had already been playing up for days because of Kevin's attitude. His appetite was suppressed, and his adrenaline output so high, that he sensed he would soon lose his cool in a most frightful way. The production manager's behavior annoyed him almost daily of late. Few of his staff had ever seen George angry, but when it finally happened, it was not all that pleasant to be too close to their employer's workroom.

Then, Friday's mail arrived. There were so many checks; the firm's financial troubles were instantly over. Everyone they knew must have loved them so dearly that they felt like paying their bills. It was as if all their customers had communicated with each other and fully understood the firm's urgent need.

Amongst the checks in the stack was one of the biggest George would ever put into his business trading account. He laughed almost all the way to the bank. But he had had enough of the factory for the week.

Barnard was on his way home early that afternoon, to take the financial pressure off poor, neglected Jodi and to spend some time playing with his children. They had missed their dad, his jokes and his tricks. It had been obvious for weeks. The telephone would be left off the hook for the rest of the afternoon. "For once, miserable old Kevin can sort things out for himself," Barnard grumbled.

Much of Kevin's considerable technical expertise was imported into the firm. But for his previous boss treating him so very badly, the conscientious though overcautious Weiss would have never joined Barnard. He would have stayed with his old firm. Their loss was Barnard's gain. But if Kevin ever managed to fully mature, he would surely owe that in part to the half-Dutch, half-French "damned impossible mongrel" migrant, George Mathieu Barnard.

⌒

"Now listen, all you kiddies!" George shouted just as soon as he walked through his front door. Instantly they came running. "I've got some wonderful news to tell you." He paused to create suspense, and decided to carefully count them: "One . . . two . . . three! Aha! All present."

All eyes and ears, they waited, eager to hear the news, suspicious of another of his regular stunts. They were clearly holding their breaths.

"We have worked *so* hard," the father told them. "And we have made *so* much money! And we loaded all the money into a huge truck. We transported it all to the bank.

Now the bank is full. No room for the people even! We are now so incredibly rich, we don't have to go back to work. Ever!" He gave them time to visualize the scenario. Then, he casually but pleadingly asked, "You guys do believe me, don't you?"

The youngest only pouted. The boy shook his head in silent disbelief. But Danielle quickly took on the task of spokesperson for the group. The verdict was loud and decisive. "We have decided! That *we* . . . will *not* . . . believe *you!* Anymore!"

"Too bad. So sad," he told them all, shaking his head and looking sorry. "That is a crying shame. You see, if all that money is not in the bank, we can't afford to go to the beach this weekend."

Quickly, like three little accomplices about to commit an underhanded act, they rushed into a corner of the room. There was a lot of whispering and giggling. Finally, they returned, and Danielle announced, "We will believe you. But only this time."

"So? All that money is in the bank?" George inquired.

"No, Daddy," Danielle answered.

"No, Dad," her brother informed him.

"Uh-uh," said the little one.

"What? What? What?" he cried, trying hard to put a look of great consternation on his face. "Our money is not in the bank? Oh, no! There goes our Sunday at the beach! What a disaster. . ."

"It's all there, Daddy," Danielle assured him with a laugh.

". . . all in the bank," the boy quickly agreed, with a hopeful look in his eyes.

"Ah?" made the smallest one. By now, she had clearly lost track of what was going on and which way to vote; one could tell by the confused look on her face as she urgently searched the faces of her siblings. A day at the beach was something that should not be missed. Any pleasing answer would do, just to get there, but what could that answer be?

A priceless reaction!

"Thank heavens it's all in the bank," George told them all. "I was so looking forward to a nice day at the beach." It was difficult not to laugh.

I just purchased three, no, two and a half opinions for the expenditure of a day in the sun, he thought, congratulating himself. When the need is great enough, anyone will believe anything.

But the whole gang swiftly disappeared into a bedroom, and their boisterous laughter could be heard, off and on, from behind the closed door, and for the next hour, as they convinced each other they had won. Fooled their father, too. This time.

"What does Simon . . . oops! What does Simone say about going to the beach on Sunday?" George asked at the evening meal.

"She says she will come, too," Danielle answered, "but the tree is going to fall on the house." Her last remark had been so unemotional, so unreservedly casual.

I live in a different time slot, the father thought. I go and whiz around this universe, looking at the future, and I do a second-rate job in coming back. I'm getting the same dumb, unbecoming answer to the question I asked last weekend. Either that or I'm hearing a strange, long-distance echo. I may be a week out of sync with the rest of the world.

"Leave your dinner, young lady," he told her. "You, and I, and that big tree over there, are going to have a lengthy discussion."

As he stood and headed for the door, Danielle slipped down from her chair and followed him. Through the door and down the steps, across the driveway and up the garden steps, then across the expanse of their finely mown lawn, they finally reached the Eucalypt. There, father and daughter faced each other beneath its wide crown. The child was wearing a most thoughtful but somewhat distrustful look.

"This here tree is a White Eucalypt," George told her as he tapped the bark. "It has been standing right here for a long time, even before you were born. It told me just recently that it likes this particular spot and it does not want to leave us. It's happy to be part of our family and it grows thousands of leaves out of sheer delight. It's a clever tree. When there is a drought, it will let some branches die. And when the rains come, it grows new branches. This tree can actually prune itself. Smart, eh?

See those dead branches up there? The tree let them die, years ago, when there was no rain."

The youngster stood staring at the foliage, spotted some dead branches, and nodded energetically.

"So, Danielle Yvette Barnard, you tell me why this blissfully contented, psychologically well-adjusted, emotionally stable tree of highly superior intelligence, standing here, holding its breath, waiting to see if you might perhaps acquire a liking for green beans, should hop all the way across the lawn to jump on your house."

Always ready to enjoy yet another of her father's impossible stories, Danielle had listened attentively and not missed a beat. She spared him a genuine smile for his effort, but she seemed hardly impressed. Pointing at the White Eucalypt, she said, "It's not *this* tree, Daddy." She turned on her heels and pointed to another tree. "It's *that* tree," she said. "Simone said so."

She was keeping her little finger pointed at a towering Gray Eucalypt that leaned slightly over the homestead. Its massive crown provided shade from the hot summer sun for all the bedrooms, as well as the living areas, of the Barnards' sizable home. Around twenty tons of potential calamity stood poised, ready to crush all occupants, should a northwesterly squall decide to write their death warrants. Only George's clinic would remain untouched, but the family might all be dead.

She looked up at her father, to see if he was paying attention, but George was stunned into silence. It felt as if a cold hand had reached into his chest and was squeezing his heart to stop it from beating. That little finger was still pointing at the Gray Eucalypt. She was waiting for an acknowledgment from the man.

But George was listening to a loud inner voice,

telling him, ordering him, "You have less than a week to down that giant, George Barnard, and you are going to contact a tree doctor now." The hair on the back of his head and neck was bristling up with the knowledge that this was a deadly serious matter.

"You go and finish your dinner, young lady," he told Danielle. "Tell Mom your father is going to have a talk with a tree doctor." He made his way to the clinic, shaken, but determined to make his call in private and to smartly get someone's attention.

That big tree had to go.

Shortly after the Gray Eucalypt episode, the Simone phenomenon simply evaporated into thin air. There were now only five places set at the Barnards' dinner table. With the arrival at Danielle's school of a new classmate, Simone—a flesh and blood version to be sure—there no longer seemed to be room for the invisible Simone, who for more than four years chose to share a meal with the Barnards, and was reported to "really, really, really and truly" enjoy, as well as need, their company.

Was Simone a simple concept born from the mind of an imaginative child—or some form of reality? Who knows? The jury may well be out on this kind of thing for another thousand years.

But George still questions: Why? Danielle and her brother were constant companions, inseparable playmates—thick as thieves, one might say. They were what he termed call-just-one-and-two-come-running children. And disagreement between these two was an absolute rarity. It could hardly have been loneliness that had triggered the birth of an imaginary playmate. Some other need? Or a budding psychic ability?

Only time would tell.

But at a time when her father was stressed to the limit, his psychic capacity utterly dysfunctional, urgent and most essential psychic information was passed on via the daughter.

They would all soon learn how they had cheated death.

2

The Gray Eucalypt

By some form of coincidence, the Yellow Pages fell open to the right page. For some reason, George unwittingly picked the first name his eyes fell upon. And by some stroke of luck, the telephone was almost immediately answered by a real person, not some dumb answering machine, even though it was after five-thirty in the afternoon— and on a Friday!

In the rush to get the attention of someone —anyone—who could take that Gray Eucalypt down, the father feverishly moved like a machine, a robot, a servomechanism, programmed to protect his family. Surely, nothing else could have existed in his mind.

Not until many weeks after the event did he begin to realize what had happened. And he needed to sit down and think about it all. "My God!" he heard himself say. "George Mathieu Barnard, what a stupid clod of a slow learner you are! The Spirit Guardians have worked ever so hard to make you take notice."

Douglas Shannon, tree surgeon, sounded tired but friendly enough. He would be around forty years of age, perhaps a little younger. His deep voice sounded like that of a confident man, a decision maker.

"You caught me in the nick of time, Mr. Barnard," he informed George. "I was about to close up shop for the day. Two minutes from now, and the gate would have been locked, and I would have been contemplating a large, cold beer."

Shannon listened to George's directions, then he cut him short. "I know exactly where your hobby-farm thing is," he commented, "because I grew up around there when it was practically all still bush. I probably know that very tree. My whole crew will be working most of the weekend, and we will be less than three miles down the road from your place. We are snowed under with work, and the electricity people are pushing us to complete the job so they can hook up another farm."

He paused. "Does your farm carry livestock?" he asked.

"Two cats, one dog, a duck, two geese, three goldfish, and a pony," George told him. "Then there is this huge herd of freeloading kangaroos."

"Bloody city farmers," Shannon laughed. "Are you growing anything, harvesting anything from the place?" he wanted to know.

"Oxygen," George told him, "lots of it. Ten hectares were cleared when we got here. The rest is covered with trees, all individually adopted by us, and they can stay. We love trees. But one of them is no longer welcome in this family. We're divorcing that one."

"Those bloody city farmers," Shannon repeated. He was enjoying himself.

Serious broad-acre farming might well be in his background, George thought.

"I'll tell you what I can do," Shannon said. "I will come and look at your tree first thing in the morning, but it will take us a fair while to drop her, if she needs taking out. I will see you around six-thirty."

Again he paused. "Now, you had better get yourself ready, Mr. Barnard," he told George in a most solemn tone of voice. "Start thinking about herding up, and fencing out, your extensive numbers of livestock." He laughed. "Those city farmers. . ." He rang off.

⁓

"Your dinner is back on the stove, George," his wife informed him. "What did the tree man say?"

"There is good news and there is bad news, Jodi," he told her. "He will come and look at our tree tomorrow. That's the good news. Now for the bad news: The man is a heathen! He gets out of bed before six in the morning, just like you do. That's revoltingly unchristian! He simply refuses to sleep when civilized people are still in bed."

"That's a matter of opinion, Barnard!" she answered him, gruffly. Despite the children's laughter, she was pinning him down with a long, cold, disapproving stare.

"I will need to break all the rules tomorrow morning," he told her, "and get up before six, *and* be fully awake. I will need to convince him to fell that tree, quick smart. It's urgent. Danielle and Simone have got it right. And I can feel it in my bones. You had better try very hard to bring me back to the land of the living, like . . . really early."

She nodded pensively. "It makes such lovely shade, that tree, and it nearly covers the whole house. We will miss it."

"With a bit of luck, it will miss us, too—on the way down, that is—if he can get it to flip over the other way. Otherwise, it *will* cover the whole house. Until then, remember you were once a Christian, and keep saying your little prayers, Jodi," George suggested.

"Never a dull moment in this household," she complained. She was giving him that tired, life-can-be-a-struggle look, but he knew she was only having a shot at him, and, likely, a shot at the Spirit Guardians, as well. "Lord only knows what we're in for next."

"Don't complain," he warned her. "A decent fright at regular intervals gives you smooth skin, less freckles, and it reduces your pimples, too."

"I don't have any freckles or pimples," she muttered.

"Shows you it's working already," he assured her.

George was the only one still finishing his sweets, but they were all still at the table. The children had missed him. It was so obvious.

Their mother liked order; George brought confusion and disorder into their lives. But kids love chaos—at least the Barnards' children always did. Their father was also, unmistakably, reading their mother's mind.

"You fool around endlessly," she complained. "Stop and think about what you are doing to these kiddies' minds. You are confusing them . . . utterly. It's a wonder they remember who they are when they wake up in the morning. It's a miracle these two find their way home from school and kindergarten, with all the crazy stories you tell them about lots of money in the bank and things like that. One day, George Barnard. . . one day, you will need to tell your children something really important, and they won't believe you at all."

"My father tells fibs," the little one chimed in, with that absolute integrity of a three-and-a-half-year-old, "all the time. But not when he says, 'I'm serious, kid!'"

George turned to the little sprite who still needed two pillows on her chair to raise her chin above the table. "What did I tell you about listening to grownup people's talk, nipper? Eh? Your ears will grow as big as my hands, furry and pointy, and they'll flop about in the breeze."

She gave him a cheeky smile because he had not said he was serious.

"That's just what I mean," the mother explained. "George, that's the kind of story that makes them all want to sleep with the lights still on."

Jodi Barnard was worried about that Gray Eucalypt, first and foremost. She was simply having a shot at him. She, herself, often enough joined in the fun, but the mother was on edge, worried about her brood. She did not have her husband's confidence in the Spirit Guardians. She couldn't have that confidence. She didn't know any Spirit Guardians.

"We might get lucky, Jodi," he suggested. "Lots of clowning around might develop their brains, their minds, and they might even acquire a sense of humor."

"We already have a sense of humor!" the boy heatedly interjected. His looks were dead-set serious, almost angry.

"Progress being made," the father told him, trying hard not to laugh, and succeeding admirably.

Only Danielle appeared to be appreciating the ironic aspects of her brother's behavior and outburst. She was rolling around on the floor now, laughing and holding her belly. Her mom had missed the point entirely.

Having Gray Eucalypts in the family, it seems, can cause lots of stress to mothers.

The converted army "Blitzwagen" had bumped its way into the home yard.

"Thanks for coming," George told the two men in the cabin.

The driver was obviously the boss, and he appeared to have no intention of either switching off the noisy engine or hopping down to terra firma. He seemed somewhat rushed and preoccupied. His voice was terse as he said, "Was it you I talked to last night?"

"Yeah, sure was, Doug!" George shouted to make himself heard.

"Which tree, mate?" Shannon wanted to know.

"That Gray Eucalypt, next to the house," Barnard answered loudly.

Shannon casually glanced at it. "Nothing wrong with that!" he barked. "I'm busy! We're going. I'll see you later!" He moved to put his stubborn old vehicle into reverse gear, but the gears just wouldn't engage.

"Doug! *Eh, Doug!*" George was shouting as hard as he could to make himself heard over the clamor of grating gears. "You've come all this way! Can't you at least take a good close look at it? Just to make sure?"

From his perch up in the cabin, Douglas Shannon looked down on him as if his patience were being sorely tried. His expression seemed to be saying something quite familiar to George's ears—something about city farmers, and hobby-farm things.

Getting out of bed so early in the morning, George mused, has got to be unhealthy after all. I knew it! What happened to the congenial Douglas Shannon I spoke to last night? He left his sense of humor under his pillow in the rush to get away.

Finally Shannon stalled his engine, grabbed up a large screwdriver, and came down to earth. His young friend stayed in the cabin, grinning from ear to ear. His staying there was a statement: "Hobby farmers know nothing."

Talking to no one in particular, the tree doctor moved all around the tree, prodding it with the screwdriver, and with great force. He was saying, "Nothing wrong. . . Nothing wrong here. . . That's okay. . . Bloody nothing wrong. . ." He levered up a large section of bark and made a great show of straightening his back. "There's nothing bloody well wrong with your tree, Mr. Barnard!"

George took his time to answer him. "Doug, my little girl tells me this tree is going to fall on the house. And when she says this tree is going to fall on the house, then that is what it will do. It will *fall*. And it will *land* on the *house.*"

Shannon was losing his cool. "We're *all* bloody experts!" he cried out. "What a load of bullshit!" The angry, frustrated tree surgeon grabbed hold of the loose bark and ripped off a strip to well above their heads.

"Ker . . . *rist!*" he shouted. As a shower of little white insects landed on their heads, the two men jumped out of the line of fire. Urgently, they brushed the tenacious, biting little pests from their bodies and clothes.

"*Shees* . . . sus!" said Shannon. Then he stood there in a long, purposeless silence, watching a stream of tiny "timber workers" as they continued to fall in their thousands from a gaping big hole in the monster Gray Eucalypt. Finally, he rediscovered his tongue. His humor as well, so it seemed. "You told me your name was George?" he asked.

"George Mathieu Barnard. That's what my momma always called me, Doug."

"Well . . . George Mathieu Barnard. . ." he drawled. "I think this tree is going to fall on your house."

"It kind of . . . looks like it," George suggested. He could do that drawl just as well as Shannon could. "What are you . . . uh . . . going to do about it?"

"We can't fix her. It's a shame. She still looks good, but she's too far gone. There are millions and millions and millions of them up there. She's had it. We'll have to cut her down."

He stepped back some more from the trunk and looked up at the foliage, still shaking his head in disbelief. "You would never know. They have done all that in the space of a year, I tell you, and she's only months away from dropping all her leaves. You know, you could have built a whole house out of what these little blighters have chewed up. What a shame. . ."

He paused. "I could have never picked it," he admitted. "And your wife knew?"

"No, my little girl knew," George corrected him. "My daughter, Doug. That's her, way over there in the sandbox, in her red jumpsuit. She's probably fabricating some breakfast for me right now. The child simply looks at what will happen tomorrow when it is still yesterday. It's a bit spooky, but it's handy to have her around. She has the Gifts of the Ancients. That's what we sometimes call it."

Shannon had once again lost his tongue. He was looking at Barnard in disbelief, but since George would only smile and nod his head, the tree doctor must have finally understood it had truly been petite Danielle who had sounded the alarm.

"Feed her regularly," Shannon suggested, "and when she gets to be twice that size, send her around. I'll give her a job." He turned to the young man in the Blitzwagen. "Rodney! Get your lazy butt out here! Something worth looking at!"

He turned back to George. "That's my son and heir. I'll trade him with you for your little girl." Then he smiled. "I'm joking, mate. He's a good one, our Rod."

"When can you cut her down?" George asked.

"In a week. When we're finished down the road," the tree doctor answered.

"No way, Doug. I want her down today. I'd like you to do it, but I will get someone else if I must. I can't ask my family to keep living under that booby trap."

"You're right, I wouldn't either. Tell you what—we can knock her down now, but we won't cart her away for at least a week. There's still more than twenty tons up there. Is that okay with you?"

"Suits me fine, Doug. Just do it." Barnard suggested.

"Rodney," Douglas Shannon addressed his son, "get the gear out pronto, or I will ask Mr. Barnard's little girl tomorrow to do it for me yesterday and in half the time."

Expertly, the two men attached a heavy steel cable around the trunk at about three and a half to four meters up from the ground. The other end of the cable was hooked onto the winch cable of their ancient Blitzwagen.

Way out in the field, well beyond danger, Rodney Shannon skillfully made the winch increase the tension on the cable. Time and again, Douglas eased the chain-saw into the massive trunk. Slowly, the insect-laden Eucalypt gained the upright position.

Holding on to their cats, dog, and goldfish, the Barnards watched from a safe distance. Their pet duck, geese, and pony were nowhere to be found. Somehow they all knew what was going to happen.

Finally, the tree leaned over the other way, bit by bit, more and more. Then she dropped, flattening the fences and shattering into dozens of huge chunks. The echoes of its eardrum-splitting impact roared and bounced around all through the valley below.

"What are we going to do with all those bits of wood, Daddy?" the little one asked.

"First up, I'm going to telephone the zoo," George told her. "We will need to borrow at least one hundred big fat South American anteaters, to lap up all those white ants."

"See you in about a week, George. And look after that little girl of yours," the tree doctor yelled, as the Blitzwagen grated painfully, then ultimately discovered its first gear. "Feed her regularly."

"She's earned her tucker for at least another week!" George yelled back. "Thanks a lot! Both of you!"

The children had spent some twenty minutes scrap-ing, spooning, and brushing the white ants into jars and tins. All that effort expended in inspired anticipation of the arrival of the anteaters. That was fun to watch! Then one of them must have remembered that their dad never told them he was serious.

"They will eat your house!" he heard Jodi argue with them. She sounded desperate. "You can't keep termites for pets! Oh, Lord, give me strength."

The clinic might well be the best place for me to hide for a while, he thought.

Kids! Chaos!

⁓

"You're just about bankrupt, George," Jodi told him with a devious smile on her face. "You've got no money and no real estate. You're out of business. And it just goes to show you that what I've been telling you all these years is right on the button: You are totally irresponsible with your money."

Petite Michelle Barnard generally, and for obvious reasons referred to as the Little One, had long ago fallen asleep on the carpet. As always, right underneath the table was her place of choice. Her siblings were wide awake, and together with the mother, they were enjoying the inevitability of George's financial demise.

"Skid row for me," he remarked, seeing no way out of the dilemma. "Out on the streets on a Tuesday night when there is a gale blowing. I haven't really lost. No, sir. I was robbed by a whole family that ganged up on me. There is the irony of it all. This is what I get in return for years of tender loving care."

"It's only a monopoly game, Daddy," Danielle tried to console him. "But Mum and I are winning and . . . we like that!"

"That's making me feel so much better," he told her. "Your concern for my welfare has made my day. It touches my heart."

Moments later, a powerful gust of wind was unleashed on the homestead. Doors and windows shook and rattled violently. Then the storm carried on as it had been blowing all evening.

"That was it, you guys," George casually noted. "That big blast of fresh air just then, that was the moment our Gray Eucalypt would have flattened us all."

They all sensed it. They all felt it. They all knew it. There really had been no need for him to say it. But suddenly, they all felt the urge to look under the table to see if little Michelle was okay.

That was strange. Why wouldn't she be? They were all fine. For some minutes after, they were all still keeping an eye on each other. To George, it felt as though the shock of the realization of their all having cheated death had awakened some primitive, knee-jerk response—a kind of disbelief that they were truly safe.

He excused himself from the game and found a quiet place for a silent prayer. "You gave Danielle the Gifts of the Ancients. I thank You for that. . ."

Morning light revealed twenty-two smashed roof tiles strewn across the home yard by the previous evening's savage gust.

"That was it, Jodi. It came precisely from the northwest."

"I've got the feeling They like us up there, George."

A whole trainload of Spirit Guides have worked their ethereal butts off to make this turn out right. George was sure of it now. Douglas Shannon's home base was right at the opposite end of town. There was no logic in his picking one of the most distant firms to do the urgent job.

Someone knew Douglas's crew was working nearby.

"Who Are We?"

Body, Mind, Spirit and Soul,
    we occupy Time in Space,
    yet we belong to Eternity.
Experiential meets Existential.
Such complex products of Creation and Evolution.

As if caught up in an avalanche of psychic events.
Spinning head over heels and out of control
    down a never-ending mountain slope
    surrounded by the ever-present powdered snow of
    the elusive Spirit World.
Bruised and beaten creatures,
    and their victorious Spirit Selves.
He is the heir of our expanding universes.
She is rich beyond her wildest dreams.

And still, so many must ask the question:

    "Who Are We?"

part two

Eleven past Eleven

That close call with the Gray Eucalypt had greatly shaken George's confidence. He was used to picking up on potential disasters of this kind, as well as future business opportunities, with monotonous regularity. He was a psychic, and everyone who knew George Mathieu already knew about his uncanny knowledge of future events. This time, his ability to see into the future had failed him miserably, at a most crucial time, and it bothered him for many weeks.

"See those warnings as a gift from an anonymous donor," Jodi suggested with a shrug and a pout, "and don't concern yourself about when it happens or where the information comes from. You've got enough on your slate. Stacks of work if you are going to study more psychology. I wish you would reconsider about going back to university, even part time. You're spread very thin already."

Jodi Barnard would soon put the entire Gray Eucalypt episode out of her mind.

George could never do that. As a businessman and therapist, in his position as a problem solver, he dealt with causes and their effects, logic and reason, on a daily basis. If the answers weren't available, he would diligently store the information in his mind for later evaluation.

Barnard was a practical man—neither a scientist nor a philosopher, but perhaps a bit of both—too spiritually oriented to ignore any of the perplexing bits of knowledge that seemed to enter his mind as if they were carried in on the breeze, too practical to accept the notion they were without a source.

Although Danielle's personality was very much like that of her mother, there was little doubt the child had inherited her father's psychic awareness. As a youngster, George Mathieu had thought himself to be surrounded by a veritable army of Spirit Friends who told him about things of the future.

Spirit Friends, Guides, or Guardians were undeniably still a vague part of George Mathieu's life, but if they were real, where were they? Without any kind of "road map" to show him the way, his delving into the Spirit World seemed an awesome task. There was little for him to work with, except time.

Time, not space, seemed to be the realm in which his Spirit Companions made their world. Another "facet" of time appeared to be the cloak worn by the Spirit Guardians, and this cloak was hiding them from the human senses.

Ever since the Barnards had purchased a digital bedside clock, George had inexplicably been awakened almost every night. When checking the time, he would invariably find it to be precisely eleven minutes past eleven; then, instantly, he would go back to sleep.

It took him many months to realize that on the days following these strange awakenings, mysteriously, there would be some unusual pre-knowledge of events already existing in his mind.

"Perhaps," George suggested in jest to his wife, "my soul travels around to look at the future and will only travel on a precise 11:11 schedule. What a stickler-for-time soul I've got! At least a part of me likes organization, while the rest of me creates only chaos." But he knew his search had only just begun.

The work was stacked up high in the factory. As well, there were many hypnotherapy patients to treat most evenings and on weekends. The pressure was on, since many of his employees were on sick leave with a virulent strain of the flu. Theories about that Gray Eucalypt enigma and Spirit Guardians would have to wait.

3

The Vice-Regent

All of George's family regularly caught colds or flu. The children were nearly always the first to suffer, and, likely, they brought all those germs and viruses home from school, kindergarten, and the little one's playgroup. Generally, their father was lucky. He didn't get all those colds and flu, and perhaps he was too busy to bother with them.

But being so overworked, knocked about, George did catch a touch of what was doing the rounds, and with a slight fever, he retired early for the night. He would sleep it off with the help of a big glass of sickly sweet, fortified red cooking wine.

The sharp eyes of the Vice-Regent of the Local Universe were upon him. Easily three meters tall, dressed in bejeweled robes, he looked awesome. George was convinced he would be shaking in his shoes, had he been allowed to bring footwear into the Vice-Regent's palace. The Vice-Regent turned to the Seraphim who were so kindly supporting the mortal. "What have you brought me?" he demanded to know. His voice sounded rather curt.

The Seraphim, invariably a twosome wherever they

are found in the star systems, spoke up in turn. "Your Gracious Honor," said the one in the electric-blue garment on George's left, in a rather deep but pleasant voice, "the carbon-based life-form before you hails from a rather insignificant blue planet. Situated at the periphery of the Milky Way, it is called Earth. It has a rather backward population of mammalian, two-legged vertebrates. This is number 483, 217, 668, 112-B, a masculine version of the species."

The Seraph in the orange gown, and to George's right, spoke next. "Your Gracious Honor," came the more feminine and friendly voice, "the Spirit Guardians of said planet have requested permission to recruit this mammal. They are seeking your permission to enroll the brute-of-a-creature into one of their platoons."

"It can't even stand on its own flat feet," the Vice-Regent commented.

"It suffers dreadfully from space sickness on long, assisted flights," said the blue Seraph. "The creature is running a very high fever. However, it travels unassisted through all facets of time, and at thought/speed within its own limited realm, because it fully comprehends the eternity/time reality differential. It has also accepted eternity/think: that we were, are, and always remain, each other."

"How interesting!" the Vice-Regent commented. "It has some borderline ability, but it looks extremely ordinary. I'm rather disappointed with its mode of dress." He was pulling up his big nose at the groggy, energy-depleted human wreck.

"We lifted it, as is, from its resting place while it slept, Your Gracious Honor," said the orange Seraph. "This is its natural outer layer. It is in fact quite naked."

George looked down to find he was indeed totally naked. Instinctively, he tried to cover his private parts with his hands, but he couldn't move. Of necessity, it seemed, the Seraphim kept a strong grip on his arms. Oh, well, he thought. Seen one, seen them all. What would this Vice-Regent know? He doesn't even have reproductive capabilities—a product of Creation, not evolution, he is. He might even be jealous. He should study good old Freud and his penis envy ideas. Good one! Crack-up! the mortal thought.

But the big "man" in the bejeweled robes had read the bedraggled human's mind, and his face had turned a bright red. He might soon throw a fit if George wasn't careful. There was anger in his eyes, thunder in his voice: "It has a bad, bad attitude," he growled.

"We are forced to live there," the blue Seraph commented dryly. "Trust me, Your Gracious Honor—on that unenlightened, chaotic sphere, sadly, they are *all* like that. They are uncontrollable!"

George was thinking, Yeah! I love being uncontrollable! I love chaos!

"Show me the paperwork on this consignment," the Vice-Regent grunted.

Seemingly from nowhere, there appeared a two-legged reptilian-like creature. It was less than a meter tall, with huge, dark, wise eyes. George thought he had seen some of them before. Companions! But where? In a dream? A nightmare? On a space journey?

Quickly, its long fingers snatched the tattered notes from the orange Seraph and handed them to the Vice-Regent for him to read. George could see there were lots of finger marks, inkblots, and crossed-out words on the standard application form. Every one of the Spirit

Guardians, it appeared, had changed something on his form. But they had all signed it. I *knew* it! Hah! Spirit Guardians are always united in their endeavors.

"This consignment is half Dutch, half French, and lives in Australia," the Vice-Regent mumbled. "It wouldn't know what, or where, it was! It owns a manufacturing plant, practices as a healer, and it studies the minds of its own deplorable species."

He carried on: "It wouldn't know what it was doing at any given time!" He went on to read, "Spirituality: Irreverent . . . but open-minded? Intelligence: Poor . . . but studies hard? Moral values: Honest and trustworthy . . . but not in amounts exceeding $100,000 of their local currency?" Grim-faced, he looked down on George. "This shipment is of no use whatever!" he exclaimed.

George wondered who had written all that on his form. That was so unkind! He knew he was honest right up to $200,000 of the currency. At least! Well . . . perhaps somewhat less.

"There are some personal notes from the Spirit Guardians attached, Your Gracious Honor," said the blue Seraph.

The big, important "man" went on to read, "We, the Spirit Guardians of the Earth's Unseen Realm, recommend recruitment of the mortal 483, 217, 668, 112-B, male, locally known as George Mathieu Barnard, into one of our progress platoons. He is a pig-headed, opinionated perfectionist, and as such, most useful to us. Cheerful under difficult circumstances, simply because he doesn't know any better, he continues to try hard to develop a sense of humor, which he will not achieve. We want him as a platoon mascot and as a challenge. Life is dull here. We need him. He is psychic and endeavoring to communicate with us, and we like that. Please consider our request favorably."

The Vice-Regent leafed through the many pages. Then he looked up in disbelief. "They all signed it!" he cried out. "How can anything so useless be popular? And this is not a request! This is a petition! This is, in fact, so strongly worded, it kind of borders on . . . blackmail. It even carries the official seal of the United Spirit Guardians' Corporation!"

He needed to think. He once more pulled up his nose at George's "mode of dress" and appeared to have made up his mind. "If they want the creature that much, they can have it. Take it out of here. Send it back. Economy class. Save yourselves the trouble. Use the catapult."

George knew what the horrible thing looked like, even before he saw it—a giant version of the one he owned when he was a kid. *Might this all be a dream?* It all seemed so real.

"Sorry, George," said the orange Seraph.

"Sorry, George," said the blue Seraph.

He was lying face up in the steaming-hot palace courtyard, about to be flung back into space. He couldn't get up. He was so ill with the space sickness and perspiring profusely with the fever. His head was throbbing.

The Seraphim were making some quick modifications to the slingshot, looking back at him from time to time. They did not want to do this to him. George knew that. But they had their orders, and Seraphim follow orders, always.

"I'm not feeling very well, and I need your assistance on this long trip," he begged of them.

"Earth is only eleven million, eleven hundred thousand light years away, give or take a light year," said the orange Seraph. "You'll be there in a flash, George."

"We put new elastics on catapult number one," said the blue Seraph. "Your favorite slingshot."

"West-southwest of the sun places you within the gravitational pull of Earth by the time you get there," said the orange Seraph. "That's when you're on your own."

"Close your eyes and hold your breath as you pass the sun," said the blue Seraph.

He was fired into space, and immediately he could feel the heat of the sun. He was already there! Space was shaking. His body was shaking. "I'm so hot," he complained. "I'm so hot. I'm so hot. I'm burning up. . ."

"You *are* burning up!" shouted a familiar voice. "Oh, God, Jesus help us!"

Vaguely, George wondered who could be living so close to the sun. Whoever she was, she might have her eyes burned out if she opened them. She would get her lungs scorched if she were breathing in. He would keep his eyes closed. He wouldn't breathe. No way! There seemed to be lots of people living near the sun. What a noisy place was this sun!

"Here, soak this! Quick! Quick, Danielle!" sounded that voice again. He knew it was a loud voice, but he could scarcely hear it.

Rivers on the sun? What a cute idea. He was feeling better now. Or maybe he was dying? Did it really matter? Probably not. At least his head was no longer throbbing. Although his eyes were closed, he could see a light in the distance. Over there would be a nice place to live, he thought. He was going there right now.

Rain on the sun? Why not? He could feel it on that body he used to own. It would certainly enjoy a rainstorm. It would also feel good, just like George himself.

"Breathe, you slob!" shouted the voice right into his ear. "Open your eyes! Open your eyes! Open your eyes and breathe, you stupid clod! Don't you dare die and leave me, you fool!" That voice sounded desperate, but so very far away.

Cautiously he opened his eyes. His wife, Jodi, was living on the sun! She was sponging him down.

"Don't burn your good nightdress," he told her. "It's very hot here."

"You were throwing one almighty fit!" she was shouting at him. She was out of breath and crying with fear. "You were damned well kicking the bucket!"

"They catapulted me back," he vaguely disagreed, "and the Spirit Guardians all signed my application form." He had peeked at the red waxen seal of the United Spirit Guardians' Corporation.

"You're delirious, raving with the fever, and those damned imaginary Spirit Guardians of yours have had you for fifteen, twenty bloody years by now. Jeez! Now, drink this!" she ordered.

Cold water on the sun? he thought. I would have never believed it if I hadn't tasted it. "Lucky you didn't burn your favorite nightgown."

Wow! She almost lost that, he thought.

"Go back to bed now, Danielle," Jodi said. "Daddy will soon be okay."

⌒

A few days of reduced working hours soon had him back on track. Only Kevin Weiss knew that his employer had to contend with sporadic epileptic fits of this kind, the result of a severe mugging, already so long ago. As far as everyone else was concerned, George Barnard could have been anywhere, selling up a storm. No one had questioned his whereabouts during the previous week. They knew he always worked long hours. Things were back to normal, as normal as they ever got.

"Almost all of us are working this evening," Kevin was telling his boss. "Are you?"

"No way. That last epileptic blow was a doozie, Kevin," George answered, "and inescap-able. The fit causes overheating, but overheating, apparently, can also trigger a fit. I only had a slight fever, but it was enough. You missed out on a promotion, son. General manager of this firm! But not by much. Keep hoping."

"Christ! Go home," he told George. "I don't want the bloody job. Not like that, if at all. You've got hypnotherapy patients tonight, if anyone asks me."

Barnard left. Had he stayed, he would have missed all the fun.

4

"Eureka!"

Life in the Barnard household had gone back to normal. The children and their mother had beaten the flu. There were no patients for George to look after that evening. What luck! Time to have fun.

Barnard was making his way home, thinking of spending a pleasant evening with his tribe. One sure way of creating pandemonium in the household was to tell the children one of their favorite bedtime stories, but to slightly alter the plot. In the past, this stunt had worked like a charm. It tended to cause a riot, with all three noisily vying for a chance to tell the original story as it really was.

"I'll stir these children up," he grunted as he pulled up to the intersection and waited for his chance to turn off. The traffic on Ring Road Three was almost bumper to bumper. Even to himself, Barnard sounded as if he were threatening his gullible offspring. "Controversy and challenges," he carried on, "will develop their little brains and minds. Yeah! I'll spur these kiddies on."

In the traffic lane next to him, a young woman in an open sports car was also waiting for a chance to merge with the traffic. She was looking closely at the man in the V8 beside her. He was sitting there . . . smiling! And talking to himself!

"That's what you've got waiting for you. . ."
Barnard told the wide-eyed woman, sparing her a
devious grin, ". . . when you get to be my age."

"Oh, God! No!" she cried. Then she
laughed.

The reins of Danielle's pony were wrapped around
the home-yard gate. Ever so slowly, so as not to spook
her skittish animal, Barnard slowly edged the V8 past the
little mare.

Jodi Barnard, her face flushed with anger, was pac-
ing the homestead patio. The Barnard's blonde, blue-
eyed eldest was receiving a severe tongue-lashing. Head
bent forward, and wiping her tears with a grubby little
hand, the distressed youngster stood there in silence.

"If I told you once, I told you a hundred times, two
hundred times, even!" shouted the angry mother. "Do
not wear your silver bangles when you ride your horse!
What will your grandmother say?"

"What disaster has befallen us now?" George
inquired.

As the mother turned to answer him, the girl quickly dashed inside, most likely to the relative safety of her
room.

"Phe-ew!" the father sighed. "The vibes around here!
You can pick them from the air and actually chew on
them. How bitter they must taste. Try one." He threw her
a handful of fresh air. "Sink your teeth into that, girl."

"She's lost her chain and bangles," Jodi complained.
"Riding that horse and wearing her best jewelry. . . Kids!
Gosh! Give me strength."

"That silver thing with clogs and windmills and tulips on it?" he asked. "Who needs it, Jodi? Who cares?"

"I do! And she should!" his wife blurted at him. "It's a present from your mother. It's got sentimental value. It could be anywhere on that ten-hectare field. She's been all over it with that horse."

"It's a mare, and a pony," George informed his wife. "It is not even half a horse. And I'll find that silver thing in a jiffy." He wondered where that last suggestion had come from. It was probably just another one of those ideas that had blown in on the breeze.

"It'll be dark soon," she objected, "and I've got dinner ready."

"I'll find it in a flash, woman." *There, I've said it again. Why?*

"We'll all go out there tomorrow," she insisted. "We'll cover the field systematically. That old dead grass is much too high. And in this light you won't have a chance."

"I'll have it in a tick." He left Jodi standing there, walked down to the field, and slipped through the barbed wire fence. Aimlessly, he walked some thirty paces.

"That was one of the most stupid things you ever told anyone," he mumbled to himself. This is a mighty big area to cover, he thought. It's getting dark and that dead grass is much too tall. How dumb can I get, saying I'll find that useless thing? My brain must be dying, softening . . . jellifying. I'm losing the bloody plot. That last epileptic fit. . . He walked a few more paces.

"Eureka!" A loud voice sounded in his right ear. He looked in its direction to see who might have said that unusual word. There was no one to be seen. He had

heard that strange word before, but he didn't know what it meant. Who's Eureka? he wondered. Some Spirit Guardian announcing its presence? It had distinctively been the voice of a male. "Send me a stunning-looking female Spirit Guide for a change," he joked. "Jodi won't mind. She won't mind about what she doesn't believe in."

He walked on for some thirty more paces.

"*Eureka!*" The voice had come back. But this time it had emanated from within his brain. It had made him jump.

"Cut it out!" he demanded of the voice. Then he laughed somewhat nervously. "Voices in my head bother me, you see. It's a leftover problem related to some serious childhood traumas. People say it isn't normal. It's mentally unhygienic, especially for psychology students, clinical hypnotherapists, and company managers. Go fool around with someone else's mind."

He stood there looking at the setting sun. It was momentarily resting on the horizon, precisely, and it glowed a beautiful bright red because of the smoke of some small bush fires far away. Fascinating! He turned to look at the homestead. It looked so picturesque at this time of the evening. He had not yet seen it from this angle without the massive Gray Eucalypt beside it, and never in this unusual light. We really do own a beautiful home, he thought. The perspective appeared to have acquired extra depth. But George was wasting time.

He was beginning to believe the search for the chain and its silver charms would have to wait. There were too many hectares of tall grass to comb, and too few minutes of remaining sunlight.

The last rays of the setting sun briefly highlighted the jewelry. Suspended by some stalks of grass, almost underfoot, the chain was intact, the bangles all there. Only the catch had come undone.

"Thanks, Eureka," he told the mystery voice. He so hoped the owner hadn't left with a chip on his shoulder for being told off. "Jeez, you saw that a long time before I did. You saw it when I couldn't have seen it because that big bunch of grass was in the way. For sure it was! Thanks, Eureka! You're ever so kind." He smiled at the thought. "Eh! Come and have dinner with us all. My treat."

"From now on, Danielle Barnard, this bracelet must take up temporary residence in your jewelry box when you ride your pony," he told the youngster sternly. "Go put it in there now, then park your animal in her yard."

The girl was utterly delighted. The mother visibly relaxed as well, for she found the chain and charms to be intact.

"And don't thank me, young lady," he told her as she made for her room to put the bracelet away. "Thank Eureka. He was already waiting for me there. He saw it first."

⁓

"Isn't it wonderful?" he suggested to Jodi later that evening. "No sooner have I decided to find out more about those Spirit Guardians, and one comes around and introduces himself. But I never heard his voice before. He's got to be new at the job. . . Eureka? Sounds Greek. I wonder what it means, that name. And why didn't I already sense he was coming this way? He sure caught me by surprise. Although . . . there was an eleven-eleven wake-up call last night."

"I found it!" she suddenly yelled at him. Then she started laughing at his frowning, inquiring glance, "That's what it means! It means . . . *I found it!* Everyone born in this country knows that. Hah! Only dreamboat foreigners like you. . . Hah! Hah! Hah! Only imports like you . . . hah! European rejects . . . hah! But people who read our history books know. People who read books on gold prospecting know. Look at all this junk. . ."

She walked over to his bookshelves. "Psychology, psychology, psychology," she said. "It's all junk! Hypnosis, hypnosis, hypnosis. All of it rubbish! Printing, photography, engineering, machine manuals, financial reviews, the stock market, the racetrack. . . It's all study material. It's all crap!" She stood there, still laughing at him.

"That still explains nothing," he told her. "Now I still don't know who actually found it, Jodi."

That remark started another uncontrolled bout of laughter. She was doubling over with her private jokes. There were times he didn't know what to think of this strange woman he had married long ago. But likely she was still abreacting the stress of nearly losing him because of that fit.

"You!" she finally shouted at him. "You did! You found it! George, you went out there, you saw it, you picked it up, and you brought it back. But you might have had just a little bit of help from Eureka."

She was laughing again, picking up his psychology magazines and throwing them at her husband. "You are such an idiot, Barnard," she said, throwing more magazines. "God! You are such a *fool!* You wouldn't know where you were living." More magazines kept coming. "Slingshots in outer space!" she laughed. "Bloody rivers on the sun!" Still more magazines were flying at him, and with speed. "You wouldn't know what was going on in this world."

She picked up another big stack, ready to throw more, but she twisted her shoulder. She looked to be in great pain, but she wouldn't stop laughing.

Much later that evening, she was still having fun about "that elusive Spirit Rascal who called himself Eureka." She was obviously also in great pain. Finally, she wandered off to bed, leaving him to sort out all his magazines and threatening to sue him for every penny he owned, and would ever earn, if the damage to her shoulder were to become permanent.

George Barnard had some thinking to do.

Already quite old at the time, but a man of great spiritual progress, Professor Doctor Edward Willis had often stressed that one's Spirit could be clearly heard. He claimed he could hear the opinions of his Spirit Self within his own mind—what he also called the Spirit's voice—simply piped into his ear.

For George Barnard there had been so many voices with important information, for so many years. He never knew who was conveying the data to his mind. Could it have been that his own Spirit Self—long ago nicknamed The Eagle for "his" frequent soaring away all over the universes—had actually been successful in communicating with him, and for many years?

His very own Spirit Self's urgings might often have been mistaken for those of his Spirit Guardians. How would he know the difference? Like Jodi said, he wouldn't know what was going on in the world. There was, however, one thing that had been very much on his mind in the days following that close-call epileptic fit: his inescapable mortality.

Death was something that had long ago lost all its mysteries. He had frequently been on its doorstep, into its foyer even, and been reefed back out of its greedy clutches to do some more mortal living. But how would he put up with The Eagle, permanently, and in ever-closer association, if that broad-winged, all-seeing, sharp-minded "Bird" lacked humor?

That unvoiced concern about humor had been so much on his mind of late. The Eureka stunt could very well have been the answer. Who might now be playing tricks on George Mathieu, while George was pulling stunts on his poor, unsuspecting youngsters?

Would he ever really know?

Professor Willis might know. Willis had been one of Barnard's lecturers in organizational psychology. Privately, "Teddy-bear" Willis, as he was often referred to by his disrespectful charges, cared little about the subject he taught. He cared about people. That's why he was there. But parapsychology was Willis's area of expertise.

With luck, he might still be lecturing at the university when George enrolled for more studies.

Our Deeply Tranquil and Imaginative Mind

is like a horse-drawn wagon, its driver missing.

Aimlessly, horse and cart dawdle through the rich,
    tall grass of the endless green prairie.

There is no point of departure, no destination.

But inevitably, the wheels of this cart will drop
    into the deep furrows, the wheel tracks,
    worn into the soft prairie soil by happenings of
        the future
    and events of the past.

The horse will gladly follow this easy trail
    and any budding coach-master may now climb
aboard
    and watch the scenery and hear the sounds
    of what was already long gone in his grandfather's
time
    and what will not yet come to pass
    when her grandchildren reach her age.

part three

Looking Back in Time

To occasionally perceive an event that has not yet come to pass can be unsettling to some. Eventually, inevitably, it will be shrugged off. It must. Life goes on. Likely, there are no explanations for the occurrence, and eventually the memory is bound to be buried in the deepest recesses of the mind.

But when the perception of future events becomes an almost daily habit, and when the accuracy of intuition or visions cannot ever be denied, the ability to consider the event "just one of those things" breaks down. At least, to satisfy the inquiring mind, questions must be asked, answers must be found.

Who are we? How real is our perception of the world we live in? Is our space transcended by unseen worlds, or could time be the wild card in the deck of experiential living we've been dealt?

Perhaps, finally, what is our purpose on this Earth, if any?

From an early age, George Mathieu discarded the notion that space could be transcended whilst time remained strictly linear. The need to know was all-important; his search for answers persistent.

Theories of the reality of time were conceived, modified, and again reworked in order for him to comprehend how, to his mind, tomorrow's happenings could already be yesterday's certainties.

The long-ago experience of the well was largely the reason for his unrelenting search and his conviction that time is a major component in the equation.

5

The Well

An invisible wall gradually built up between George Mathieu and his father. Theodore Barnard, a political middleweight, a man of logic and reason, was somewhat fearful of George's remarkably accurate predictions. He tended to rubbish the boy for being a spooky dreamer of a child.

This middle child of Theodore's seven children was not like the others. But the tall, highly critical Frenchman constantly overlooked the fact that his beloved wife was just as spooky, if not a great deal spookier.

George Mathieu was tired of being referred to by his papa as the dreamer, the family's fortuneteller, or the biblical dream interpreter Joseph.

The French can be so very rough on their kids. Still, their kids are resilient. Eventually, George learned how to clamp his mouth shut about who would come to visit the family the next day. He learned not to say a word about who would be on the telephone before it rang. Jealously, and fearful of hurtful verbal responses, he learned to keep his experiences to himself.

In dealing with the phenomena, he was now quite alone.

Tentatively, most cautiously at first, "another George Mathieu Barnard" had long ago and regularly been on the loose during the night when the "little, real George" was asleep in his bed. This other George could roll down the stairs and not get hurt. He could slip through the crack under the door and sit on the living room floor until the early morning hours, listening to the grown-ups' conversations. Without being noticed, he could watch his papa write his political speeches.

Intense resentment of being sent to bed so early in the evening, one might presume, may have been the cause. Even when George was two, some aspects of what was to become a life-long night owl syndrome were already in evidence. That astral self, for want of a better term, was running wild. And he could learn things, and tell the real George about it later. It was ever so handy to be two people instead of just one.

By the age of eight, George had taken to the skies. He soon concluded there was only one of him, but this one could split himself in halves—one half could fly, the other half could only jump and was in for a heavy, painful landing from a badly judged height. The flying half could land on a roof and just sit there, or plunge through it at will, but there was a problem: If he had doubts about his future as an aviator, he had to flap his arms to stay aloft. Strong doubts kept him grounded. Confidence, however, allowed him to zoom around to his heart's content.

Talking about his flying caused a lot of loudly expressed cynicism from his school friends. For months, every effort to leave his body was in vain. But his friends all quickly forgot about it when George wouldn't talk about it anymore.

About to drift off to sleep one evening, he stubbornly refused to go all the way. Hovering between wakefulness and sleep, it finally happened: Out popped his astral self, to take along his mind and go soaring through the sky again.

This was it! The right way had finally been found. He could go anywhere at the speed of thought or float out there at his leisure. Almost every night, he whizzed around his school's playground. And being sent to bed early was no longer something to be resented. Weightlessness was better than an extra helping of ice cream for dessert.

One night, as he zapped over the wooden schoolyard fence, an obstacle that should not have been there confronted him. He stopped in mid-air, just before he would have crashed into the thing that blocked his flightpath. He hovered all around it. No doubt about it—it was a well, such as could still be found in many old places. It had no business being there because no one needed it. There were water taps inside their school building, a drinking fountain by the gate. Besides, the well looked to be quite old. Twenty-five or thirty years old it was, perhaps even older. It was in an awkward place, no more than five meters from the double back doors of his school.

He wondered who would be stupid enough to put this second-hand well right where the kids kicked their soccer ball. Not to mention this person being so dense as to forget about the chances of yet another child drowning in yet another old well. He was determined to voice his opinion about the thing when he returned to school the following morning.

Imagine his surprise to find that the well wasn't

even there! Certain he had seen it, he checked the exact spot. Sure enough, there was somewhat of a dip in the paving that could indicate there might have been a well there at some time in the past.

The discovery of that well presented him with a problem he simply could not solve. This was his second year in primary school, and he was only just trying to grasp the conundrum of simple division. What was happening to time, as he understood it?

Every second that ticked away pushed the French Revolution further back into history, sure enough. It also brought his next birthday a second closer, without doubt. But he had looked at, and touched, something that might have once been there. The problem was too massive for George to solve, but he had to know. He would dare ask older people about that well.

More than seven years his senior, his brother Antoine wanted to know what he was up to now. And if he wanted Antoine's signature on a petition for the urgent installation of one of those wells, he could wait until Antoine was old and senile, and until George himself sported a long gray beard, he was told. Civilization would suffer an unimaginable setback if George Mathieu were to be left in charge of anything. Both fire and the wheel would need to be reinvented later.

That was typically the way Antoine would respond. It simply meant he had never seen the well his younger brother was talking about.

Neither of his parents had attended that school. They didn't know about the well, they said, but logic should tell him there was a good chance that a well had been there somewhere, before water was piped throughout the town. And why did he want to know about those dangerous things?

The boy simply shrugged. No way would he tell anyone else about his astral traveling. He was determined he would never again have to flap his arms to stay aloft or risk more condemnation by his papa for being so spooky.

One of his uncles had gone to that school, but he could not remember anything about a well being there. "The school already had taps in them days," his uncle said.

George risked asking the headmaster for a moment of his valuable time, and the man had a long think about it. "I began teaching here in 1934," he said, "and became headmaster in '38. No, George. No well. But there might be one indicated on the old plans. I'll dig them up for you. Wouldn't mind finding out for myself, actually."

Mr. Bodegraven, bless his soul, was a kind man, and very clever, but shockingly forgetful. He would not remember about those plans even if he saw the boy the very next day.

Many weeks later, George was still racking his brains, planning to visit the town council, if someone could be cajoled into taking him there. The council had plans going back hundreds of years, it was said. But Jehanne Colette, or Jéjé, George's much-loved and only sister, was too timid to take him there, and George trusted no one else in the family with a further mention about that well.

Then his Mama's eldest brother, his Uncle Daniel, came to visit the family. Daniel did not think it strange the boy should know about the well. He knew what the little man's mama and grandpa were all about. "For sure, George Mathieu, that old concrete well," he told the youngster. "They filled it in with a cartload of sand, and the concrete they broke up from the well-head. Maybe 1930, '31, or '32—I'm not sure. Pavers over the top, and you'll not find it in a month of Sundays, but I'll tell you where it was. Right outside the back doors, in a straight line, give it six, seven paces. A teacher's nightmare it was on a hot summer's day, with all those kids pushing for the cold-water bucket. The teachers hated that well, and it was the strap for any rascal who came too close to it, or pushed in the queue. I might have some very painful memories. . ."

With a smile, he touched the appropriate place. "The bruises are still there, Georgie," he lied. "Some of those sores are still bleeding. You know your Uncle Daniel, son. Not one out-of-place word ever dared to slip out of my mouth," he laughed.

George's Uncle Daniel was known to have been quite a rogue. He still was one at heart, the boy thought. He talked a lot about a bucket on a rope, and how it was dunked upside down. George had never seen that bucket. His Uncle Daniel was vague about the wooden lid of that well, and its twisted wrought-iron handle, which George had inspected closely.

The youngster decided that what his uncle remembered was near enough, and he tried to figure out how he could turn up somewhere before he was born—years before he was born! It was much too difficult for him to grasp at his age. Neither could he ask anyone for help with this puzzle of time. No one would ever learn about his flying away from home night after night. He would never again flap his arms or be criticized for seeing the future, let alone the past.

It took him many years to learn how to target

precise times of the night, and even longer to learn how to leave at night and turn up somewhere in daylight. It took almost ten more years for him to learn how to leave in daylight.

Already the next problem had presented itself when he decided to clear his regular flight path and destroy that unwanted well. Sometimes it was there, and sometimes it was missing. As well, he could feel the texture of the concrete, but he would put his foot right through it if he kicked it. There was no way he could break it. It was all too difficult for him to work out.

Finally, only recently, had he come up with a theory that perfectly fit the experiences. This had to be the answer. Pleased as anything, he was. Then, another "impossible situation" presented itself almost immediately, closely followed by yet another. And these two "impossibilities" are still rattling around in his brain, looking for an answer.

Truly, our universes may hold few miracles. But there happen to be ever so many things our minds cannot handle just yet. Some of these must be due to our erroneous concepts of the complexity of time.

Since to George's mind, tomorrow's visitors to the Barnards' home could clearly be seen to be visiting the family on that day, tomorrow was already a shadowy reality. His seeing and feeling an old well that had long ago been destroyed and made safe proved to him that, in some way, time persisted in "hanging about." But George was unable to contemplate another reality of time without visualizing it as something material.

Time could be a gentle wave. The rise could be the past. The crest could be the moment of an event. The receding part of the wave could be the future. And from anywhere inside this wave, that event could be viewed—forward or backward in time—by a curious mind that darted about in this, or any other, wave. To George's mind, time was unstable, elastic, fuzzy.

Time could be a wire, stretched out into infinity. And every event was a tiny bead that slowly slid along this wire past a certain point that is "here and now." Moving back from this "here and now" point, the beads of future events would slowly slide into view. The beads of past events would casually slide away into ancient history.

The youngster needed these tangible representations of time to wrap his mind around what was happening to him. His mother was perfectly happy accrediting all of her psychic capacity to sweet old St. Christopher. What an overworked saint he was! His father denied that anything like that could exist and simply perceived thousands of "coincidences" during his lifetime. But George was like neither parent, and at the same time he was like both. Psychic things were now daily happenings, and he needed to know how they worked, and why.

For many years, he saw time as an imaginary, giant, golden coiled spring. It could not exist without motion. It expanded and contracted at will and reached into infinity. All events were engraved on its countless loops, and could be read at random as neighboring loops of the coil moved past. That coiled spring served him well.

Finally, the simultaneous realization of a cause in the distant past and its effect on the distant future blew his precious metal spring to bits. George did not need it anymore. He visualized it drifting off into deep space. And those countless tons of precious scrap metal could happily stay there.

Many theories had been adopted and discarded until, as a young man, he concluded that his mind was transcending time by "touching" eternity, where all events, past and future, were always, and already, a reality.

However, a belief that time cannot exist, or be sustained, without motion, persisted. He saw time as a manufactured product that must constantly be replenished, nourished, or maintained. But time—perhaps time together with space—is surely inhabited by unseen life forms. The youngster would soon find evidence.

Right now, as a father of three, a businessman, and a therapist, his search remains unrelenting as he takes his mind back to more events of the past.

6

"You Must Wait!"

She had come to help her dad catch a big fish, she informed George Mathieu with wide-open eyes and an air of great candor. But her all-important task was quickly forgotten. The lively, blonde, blue-eyed three-year-old in her pretty pale blue dress had discovered the tall-stemmed daisies. Quickly, she gathered as many as she could hold and then seated herself next to her dad, on the fresh spring grass nearby.

"He woves me. Pfrut!" George heard her say. "He woves me not. Pfrut! He woves me. Pfrut! He woves me not. . ." She was unstoppable.

George checked the water around his float for telltale ripples and looked across to the little girl and her father. She was pulling the white petals from the golden flower heads one by one, and, with the aid of the gentle breeze, blowing them onto the still canal.

What a sight! Saliva dribbling down her chin, she was putting an excellent effort into her newfound task, spitting and spluttering to make the petals reach the water.

Why should I bother to watch that dumb float? he thought. Watching this little sprite is much more fun. He caught the father's eye. The man was enjoying himself as well, laughing without making a sound. He smiled a knowing smile at George.

"She practices her *l*'s and *r*'s," the man commented, "every day, tirelessly. Her six-year-old sister's almost got it down pat. Now she wants to learn how to blow as well." He looked like one of those parents with a great sense of humor, who took the endless chatter of his offspring all in his stride. His face was full of the kind of wrinkles that were caused by laughing all the time, George thought.

"She's making a mighty fine job of it, sir," George agreed.

"Never gives up," the father answered proudly. "She'll entertain me all day."

George looked back at the field of daisies. There were thousands upon thousands of them! An ocean of those flowers right across that field was easily enough to keep her on the job for a week.

But he wondered if she would be loved, or not be loved, long after she knew her *l*'s and *r*'s, and when she could hygienically blow out twenty or so candles on her birthday cake to be shared around.

Someone, somewhere, already knew the score, he mused.

This would be the last time fifteen-year-old George fished in the canal he had so often visited. He was miles behind on his homework. If he didn't get a move on and study regularly, he would soon see his chances of eventually acquiring a college degree slip away. Having accepted a weekend job at the local bakery to help pay for his tuition would make it even tougher to catch up on the many essays. Fishing was out, probably for good. And the bakery was always busiest in holiday times, with the influx of tourists to their seaside village.

He checked both ways for high-speed trains on the track and diagonally crossed both the railway line and the canal over the ugly old Big Iron Bridge.

How inventive are the Dutch? he wondered, with more than a little of Papa Barnard's humorous cynicism. "If it's big, made of iron, and functions as a bridge, you call it the Big Iron Bridge. What else would you call it? Pont des Hirondelles, because the thing is chock-a-block with nesting swallows in the spring? No, you don't. Pont des Fleurs Sauvages, because the wildflowers are about as numerous as the blades of grass around there? No, you don't. Pont du Poisson Gras, because a twenty-five-kilo carp has permanently set up home under it? No you don't. You call it the Big Iron Bridge, that's what you call it."

The sharp-witted Frenchman would say things like that and laugh. But there was always more coming after that. "And the carbon copy of that ugly thing, just twelve hundred meters farther north, up the railway line, you call it the Other Big Iron Bridge. What else would you call the thing? How I love the Dutch! I even married one of the creatures!"

That would be his papa's kind of punchline.

Bridge of the Big Fish would be George's choice for this big iron bridge.

The canal below the Big Iron Bridge was no longer navigable. It still served as an irrigation channel, but during infrequent water shortages elsewhere in the system, it used to be drained in a hurry to keep the freight barges from stranding. Bad luck for the farmers. But fish would congregate in the biggest ponds, making them a little easier to catch.

That great big carp had always eluded him, year after year. The fish owned the biggest pond, right under the bridge. That cunning big scoundrel could take the bait from the hook and never even move the float. In the end, George did not want to catch him anymore.

Mama Barnard had expressed the opinion that given a choice, just as many people would prefer a plate of that big fish for its nutritional value as would fancy a dish of fresh garden soil for its superior taste. It was her way of saying, "Don't you dare drag that smelly thing home."

Somehow it no longer seemed right to catch him. And perhaps, in the young man's mind, the carp had stopped being a fish and had now become a legend, a part of George's life, a personality and a friend.

The boy was only seven when he learned about the carp, and he quickly became convinced that the one person who could pull that fish from his pond would be him—sometime, when he was old and strong enough.

One day, he would scale that almost vertical rock wall and he would be down there, below that big bridge, and catch that fish. He was ten years old when he plucked up the courage to attempt the climb. Carefully edging his way down the northeastern side of the bridge, he finally discovered a wide concrete shelf to sit on. Though dangerous, and hard to get at, it was worth the risk because of the fish he caught there weekend after weekend, and for getting the occasional glimpse of the monster carp. But the carp remained elusive.

When the high-speed trains whizzed by overhead,

the clamor was just about unbearable. One had to be quick, once every twelve minutes. Put down the rod, put your foot on it, and quickly stick your fingers in your ears. After that, you could once again relax.

⌒

He was pulling in a bass. It looked to be just over a pound—a good little fighter, and excellent for the table. Someone was shouting something at him from above. He had missed what this person was trying to tell him, but he knew the voice. It belonged to Walter Groen, the playground bully. Walter was twelve years old, not very bright but big and strong. He picked on small kids George's size, but he left his own classmates alone. Not very brave, but mean, was Walter Groen.

George pulled in the bass, moved to the edge of the concrete shelf, and looked up at the bully. "What do you want, Walter?" he shouted.

"I want you to shove off out of my fishing spot!" the big kid yelled at the top of his voice.

"Go home to your farm and milk a cow!" George shouted back. "Today, this is my fishing spot! You can have it tomorrow!"

"I will come down there and drown you, you little bastard!" Walter shouted.

Walter Groen had George concerned. He knew how this kid hit small people in their faces and gave them wobbly teeth. Offering to share the wide concrete shelf with him would do no good. Walter loved violence too much. There actually was a good chance he would drown George Mathieu.

Mucking out his father's stables had made Walter

strong. Big meals with lots of pork and dairy products had made him tall. Rough treatment by a strangely shy and chronically mentally unstable father had made him ruthless.

If George dived into the water and made it to the other side of the canal, he would be safe. But he would have to wait until Walter was more than halfway down that rock wall before diving in. That steep wall was the only way down and the only way up. George knew he could easily outswim the bigger boy. But if he stayed on his side of the canal, Walter could get back up the wall in time to grab him as he crossed the bridge. However, either way, George would lose his fishing gear and his first catch for the day. He needed to talk his way out of it.

"What makes this your fishing spot, Walter Groen?" he shouted up to him.

"I live the closest to it!"

"I live the closest to the town clock, you idiot!" George shouted back at him. "And I've seen you look at the time on it." He had made a big mistake using the word "idiot" on Walter, who knew he was somewhat of a slow learner and touchy about it. Walter Groen looked very angry about George's glib remark.

The loud, back-and-forth abuse was becoming more pathetic as it went on. Who owned the bridge? Who owned the canal? Who owned the land around it? Was it the burgomaster? The queen? God? Walter Groen was getting angrier by the minute. He was about to make the slow descent. He was going to come down to drown George Mathieu. "And how could you be a proper Dutchman ever, with a stupid name like Barnard?" he wanted to know.

"Give me five minutes!" George yelled up at him.

"I'll give you two minutes to come up here, you little rat!" Walter shouted back.

George knew that if he climbed up, he would still get bashed when he got there. Walter might even push him from the steep wall as he neared the top. George was indeed feeling like a little rat—a little rat in a trap.

"I need exactly five minutes, Walter, please," he begged of him, but he was fuming inside, for Walter Groen had insulted the name "Barnard." That was unforgivable.

The bully leaned over farther, frowning at George, "Why?" he asked almost casually.

"To put a sharp edge on my scaling knife!" George shouted, showing him the knife and pushing it across the concrete to make a loud, scratching sound. "I'll wait here for you, Walter! I'll stick it right up you where it doesn't fit!" He had declared war. Walter Groen backed off for the day, but he said he would get even. And one could always bank on Walter's vindictive, steel-trap mind.

George managed to avoid Walter Groen for almost eight months. Every time he thought himself to be in his clutches, he got away or managed to outsmart that bruiser of a kid. Twice, Walter's efforts were foiled because someone chanced to pass by at a critical moment. He was getting angrier, and George's luck couldn't last.

This time, there was to be no escape from the maltreated, neglected, revengeful boy. Walter and his younger brother, Nicolas, were waiting for George—and they would beat him to a pulp.

It was a cold day, just below freezing. By three in

the afternoon, snow still covered the dunes from the top down to the high-water mark. The sea wind and some threatening gray-green clouds to the west promised more snow for that evening and night. Already, the wind was picking up. In thirty minutes, it would be dark.

George had been beachcombing since ten o'clock that morning and he was cold and tired, looking forward to the warmth of their coal heater and a big hot meal. He had covered an enormous distance. Everything worth keeping was tied to his papa's sturdy bicycle, mostly wooden planks and three green glass floats in fish net. He presumed his dad would be pleased with him and his day's labor. It was a rich bounty for a kid of just eleven summers.

There was just one more huge, snow-covered sand dune for him to climb. It would be downhill all the way from there, towards food, warmth, company, and appreciation for his efforts. Momentarily, he stopped to catch his breath and to survey the hill. He needed to pick his way past frozen sand-slides and heaped-up snowdrifts, whilst pushing that loaded-up bicycle to the top.

There stood Walter and Nicolas Groen. But for the farmer's sons and George Mathieu, the place was deserted. There was no escape. His heart sank. He was cold and stiff, unable to run, and he would soon become one of the Dutch nation's all-time experts on the subject of extreme discomfort and pain.

The older brother's stance—his body language— said it all: "I've got you! This is not your lucky day, George Mathieu Barnard."

"You must wait!" sounded a loud, sudden warning. It had apparently come from nowhere. George stopped and looked around. There was no one! No one to be seen

but the two Groen kids some thirty meters up the hill. But this had been the do-it-or-else voice of a grown man! As well, the two would-be muggers were facing the breeze, and the sound of their talking was drifting inland, together with the first tentative flakes of another snow-storm about to hit.

Like an obedient sheepdog under orders from his master, George stood there, flat-footed. He most always did what his teachers told him to do, what his parents told him to do. But this was just a voice out of thin air! And he was doing as he was told! Blindly following an order.

He glared at the two. Cold and tired, feeling responsible for his papa's heavy bicycle and his precious "cargo," he would be no match for the brothers. Walter alone could turn him into minced meat. With Nico's help, George would be in for the mugging of a lifetime on that cold carpet of snow. But he would not go down without a fight. Given half a chance, he would sink his teeth into one of them and mark him for life. Nothing other than his sharp teeth would be of any use. He was too cold, too numb. But he waited as he was told to do, preparing for a vicious battle he knew he couldn't win.

Walter was getting restless. Menacingly, he took some steps towards George and his bike, then he stopped, turned, and spoke to his brother. He sounded loud and angry, but George couldn't catch a word of what he was saying. The younger boy seemed to be objecting about something, unwilling to follow Walter and disinclined to get involved.

That little fellow had rather a lot to say, and Walter, gesticulating angrily, tramped back up the hill to talk to him. As the young one replied, the breeze lessened somewhat, and then, momentarily, it shifted to the east. George heard him say, ". . . knows what we are going to do with him. . ." Then his words were lost as the wind once more blew from the northwest from behind the young beachcomber, drowning out the sounds. George kept his eyes on the two without moving and waited some more.

Suddenly, and to his surprise, both boys ran off and up the hill. They moved as if driven by great fear. With the two gone over the rise in a twinkling of an eye, George was left alone. When, just a few minutes later, he made it to the top with his treasure on two wheels, they were nowhere to be seen. Nowhere, on more than a kilometer of open road, could he spot their dark-colored coats. Nowhere, on snow-clad dunes as far as the eye could see, was there a movement.

"'You must wait?'" he mumbled to himself. "Wait for what?"

It is a question he has asked himself many times since that wind-chilled, late afternoon. It is an unanswerable question. He knows what happened to him. He heard an authoritative voice, telling him to wait, and that is precisely what he did. He also knows that a benevolent person, unseen, invisible to mortal eyes, watched over him.

What happened to that despicable duo is another matter. Something sure happened to them. George never saw any kid move as fast as they did, hunted up a hill like they were. Never would that playground bully pass up a chance to beat him to a pulp—not of his own free will. Would he have allowed himself to lose face when the most ideal opportunity presented itself? No way! Not this hardened youthful mugger. For Walter Groen, that would have been unthinkable. But he did! He ran!

Whatever happened to those two that late afternoon on that sand dune, George will never know. Not in this life. They never did get to be on speaking terms—Walter, Nico, and the Frenchman's son.

Their paths crossed many times after that cold winter's day, but both Walter and Nicolas gave him a wide berth from that time on.

But something must have happened.

Why else would George have had to wait?

A Spirit Guardian, Barnard presumes, saved him from a severe beating. The event reminded him, though ever so vaguely, that as a very small child he had often felt himself to be surrounded by Spirit Guardians. There were distant memories of having seen them.

Their concept of time—he now suggests with great confidence—which contains a clear grasp of the reality of eternity, does not correspond with ours. Their view of a human life may well be of its totality.

Each of our lives, from beginning to end, from birth to death, may be seen as represented by a little colored stone in the mosaic that is our collective time/space journey. A mere segment of this mosaic is the family; a portion of it is the community; the whole composition a nation, a world population.

But two of these little colored stones were working their way loose from the surface and threatening to unsettle a third, and perchance even more of the composition, as their evil plan "repercussed" into the future.

Those stones needed to be pushed back into their places in the mosaic of their time. For the third little stone, it was payback time. Simply that—no more, no less. Payment for a few "universe credits" not yet accrued.

He would earn those credits in the future as he battled to improve the lives of his fellow man and healed so very many.

It would be eight more years before George Mathieu would heal his first patient by simply touching her.

But someone, somewhere, already knew the total score.

7

Jumping The Gun

At least once per week, there was a delivery to be made to Gillies Burglar Alarms. This had become a regular task for the lone young migrant, nineteen-year-old George Barnard. It was a matter of hopping off his train one station earlier, handing the parcel to Warren or Janelle, and making his way home on foot.

It saved his employer time and money not to have to send his delivery truck into an out-of-the-way residential area, and it gave the struggling Warren Gillies his needed components a day earlier. For George, it usually meant a cup of tea, a biscuit, and a chat with Janelle. He enjoyed talking with her.

At twenty-seven, the "been there, done that" young mother was always good for another outrageous story about what she and her mates had been up to.

In her long, fringed dresses, and with her many strings of beads, she looked the part—an uncontrollably wild woman. But looks are so deceiving. She was now a wife and mother, receptionist, bookkeeper, tea lady, and messenger girl. Even then, she still found time to assemble a few of Warren's burglar alarm systems.

George much admired this industrious couple and they had also "sort of adopted" him. They thought he was presumptuous, too serious in talk-ing about a business he had not yet started, a wife he had not yet met, and a tribe of children that would not be born until years into the future.

Just of late, Janelle had been looking very pale, drained, listless.

Warren Gillies's little van was not in the driveway. He would still be out on an installation or a service call, George presumed. Janelle was not in her office either. There was no one to take his parcel or sign his delivery docket. He would wait. Janelle is probably at the corner shop, he thought. I'll switch on the jug and wash the mugs.

Then he noticed Sunshine's pram next to Janelle's desk. But baby Sunshine was now too heavy to carry all the way to that corner shop, still much too young to walk. Something was very wrong.

The room behind Janelle's office was marked PRIVATE. George had never been in there. He knocked on the door, but there was no answer. Perhaps all three had left in their van. But why not close up shop for the day? Besides, they knew George was making an urgent delivery, and they knew his train schedule.

This seemed all wrong to the young man. He opened the door to their private room. It was pitch dark in there.

"Where is that overgrown hippie?" he joked. Then George saw her.

She looked as white as a sheet and about to slide from her chair. Sunshine was on her lap, fast asleep, but about to make a tumble onto the concrete floor.

"What *are* you doing, woman?" he asked as he stepped through the door. He dropped his parcel and reached for the baby to stop her from falling.

"Take Sunny," Janelle whispered. She could barely make herself heard.

That was easier said than done. Babies don't come with sturdy handles. Even at age nineteen, George tended to give babies a wide berth. They should come with "Fragile" labels stuck all over them, he felt, right up until the age of two.

He got her at last. Now what do I do with this bundle? There was a cot in the corner of the room, and he managed to safely get the package in its little bed without dropping, or even waking, the prize.

Janelle's pale looks and weary smile said it all: "How damned hopeless are you, George Barnard?"

He returned to the mother.

"Get me off this thing," she whispered.

The way she was slung over that seat would surely break her back. George's eyes were getting accustomed to the darkness now. It seemed she had fallen onto the wooden chair. Then the young man realized what had happened. She had been sliding off it with her own blood. Her lower body was soaked in blood.

"Christ, you made a bloody mess, Janelle!" he cried.

He dragged her onto a settee and found a towel to put under her. This woman needed no "Fragile" labels. She had spent ten days sitting atop a pole in her younger years, for whatever reason kids like her spent ten days atop a pole, and in all kinds of foul weather. She was tough and bony. But she needed fluid now, urgently— water or tea—and he needed to phone an ambulance.

Find Warren Gillies. Telephone his boarding house to tell them he would be late. He would sign that dumb delivery docket himself.

Why am I so calm? Am I heartless? Here is poor Janelle, practically hemorrhaging to death, and I am refusing to panic! *This is weird.* George Barnard was robbed of all emotion. He was no longer human. He was a machine, seemingly precision-tuned to do exactly what had to be done.

"Weak black tea and a little sugar. Get it into you now," he ordered. "You've lost so much fluid."

She was sipping away at the cup and looking a little livelier.

"You've done some crazy things in the past, Janelle, but you're a little person's mother now. This might be the time. . ."

"I tried to sit down just before I fainted," she whispered. "I fainted, George, holding Sunny. God. . ."

"I'm going to ring for an ambulance now," he told her. "Keep slurping away."

But Janelle grabbed his arm and would not let go. "No," she told him. She had found her voice at last. "Just stay here with Sunny and me until Warren comes back. Lock up the shop, mate, and ring your landlady."

"You're not yet thinking straight, Janelle," he informed her calmly.

"I am. I've been springing major leaks like this, off and on, since Sunny was born," she told him. "George, I've not stopped bleeding in ten months now."

"Cripes!" he exclaimed. But he was thinking, I don't know *anything* about what she is saying. Parents don't prepare their sons for the inevitability of menstruation and childbirth. At least, not where I come from. She will need more than aquarium putty to stop up that leak. There was blood all over her chair, the floor, and her lovely dress. She needed a doctor, quick smart.

"It'll soon stop," he told her. Now, *there* was a ridiculous statement for him to make. That presumptuous remark had come from nowhere. It had shocked him. He tended to do that so often. Embarrassing!

"Give me your hands," she told the young man. That was the third time in as many weeks someone had said that to him.

A colleague of his had told him he had healing hands, and he had rewarded her with a big smile and half of his chocolate eclair. Then he had told dear old Ethel he fully agreed. His healing hands were doing an excellent job at his task of work, but especially at feeding him during meal times. And eating always made him feel so much better.

The other "enlightened" informant was called Sarasvati—Swami Sarasvati. Although the seer had told George many things about his past he could not have known, he made the mistake of becoming too excited about the young man's future as a healer. Young Barnard had no intention of getting involved with healing, not then. Sarasvati's behavior spooked and embarrassed him. He had walked out of the chance meeting with the Indian guru.

"Give me your hands," Janelle insisted.

"Don't be ridiculous," George told Janelle. "I'm nineteen; what can I do?" He wasn't at all sure about what she was going to do with his hands, or where she might put them. The woman had done some really weird things in the past.

"Give me your hands!"

She would soon burst another major pipeline, somewhere, if he didn't keep her calm. And so, he sat there like a fool, holding her head, for ten whole minutes at least.

His mind said, No, not yet—but he knew the time would come. His Spirit Self knew better, but had jumped the blast of the starting gun by more than thirteen years.

Nothing other than Janelle Gillies's faith was healing her pale, drained body. Right there, and right then, ten months of her misery came to an end. She unerringly already knew it would.

That evening, as the teenager George Barnard watched a movie, the stress of that late afternoon suddenly became too much for him.

He suffered an abrupt, horrible bout of the shakes, and this might well have been his first-ever epileptic fit—a stress-induced epileptic fit, perhaps—as he began to relax and started to realize how close to death his mate Janelle might have been, and what could have happened to baby Sunshine.

George's rather sudden, inspired decision to make his home in Australia also cut short his studies in business management. But just a little over a year after starting his own business, he was studying again.

Industrial psychology was his choice. It came in handy in his dealings with clients, employees, and suppliers. It also led him to become a qualified therapist, and it did so in a most astounding, inexplicable way.

8

"Go Check It Out"

In answer to frequent scathing comments about his ostensibly absurd combination of interests—manufacturing and psychology—George Mathieu had built a powerful defense. "The proof of the pudding," he would say, "lies in a rapidly growing and prosperous company." Case closed.

Employees were carefully selected, firstly for their suitability to repetition production. The workers were then picked with an eye to the individual's ability to function as a member of one of a number of small teams. Staff was generally happy, caring about the work, and supportive of each other; production rates were high. So was the company's profitability.

Undeniably, volume production and industrial psychology went well together.

In turn, above-average wages attracted the best in the business—the thinkers, the decision-makers, the promoters and innovators. It suited George's restless nature. Mass production of a wide range of goods beyond initial planning and design bored the living daylights out of him. He needed it to survive, but he disliked routine. He liked sales, his studies, the stock market, and the racetrack. Even in later years, the clinic and the many hours it took out of his work schedule always remained a comparable financial dead loss.

"As our company sucks the lifeblood out of the community, the clinic spits it back in," he claimed. "It helps make the world go round."

To not run the clinic would be to live a greedy, selfish life, he felt.

⁓

The psychology department was auctioning off some of its unwanted books, equipment, word processors, and computers. Psychology students had also contributed whatever they could spare from previous years' study materials and personal belongings. There was a mountain of goodies to bid on, by all present. The auction would begin just as soon as everyone had eaten his or her fill of sausage sandwiches.

Louise Hewitt, a member of George's study group, brilliantly intuitive and some ten years his junior, had found them a shady spot on the lawn. They were both finishing off the last morsels from the lunchtime barbecue.

"I'm getting nowhere with my 11:11 wake-up calls, Lou Lou," George remarked. "Every dream I have shows me the same stupid visual message: a flat box."

"Chocolates!" came her immediate but indistinct response. Then she took her time to empty her mouth, and said, "Get a really, really big box of the ones with the soft fillings and bring them to lectures with you. But let your wife and baby have some too."

Louise was not in the mood for discussing problems with dreams. She had her eager eyes on some of her next

year's study books. With little money in her purse, she
still wanted those books, and she would happily fast for
a few days to be able to obtain them. She was counting
on a fast, having just put away her fourth of the free
sausage sandwiches.

Offering the young woman a loan was a waste of
time. He had found that out long ago. This permanently
frustrated chocolate freak was far too proud and inde-
pendent to accept charity.

Someone was pulling in the crowd. People were
surging forward and there was lots of laughter. One of
their lecturers was auctioning off his secretary, and she
was loudly protesting the low starting price. Every cam-
pus surely had at least one pair of clowns like this, for
general entertainment and to get things rolling. The real
auction would now soon begin. Louise was pushing for
a better spot and searching in her purse for the list she
had made.

"What color is the box you saw in your dream?" she
suddenly asked.

"Bright red," he told her. He looked around. "See
that book on top of the stack, smack in the middle there?"
he asked. "That's about the color of it, Louise. That's
about the size of it as well, I'd say."

"Get it," she told him.

"That's what I call impulse buying," he laughed.

"Just get it!" she insisted. "You're rich, Barnard. You
can afford it." But as he showed no interest, she growled
at him, "Keep your eyes on my purse, Barnard, you slow-
moving thing."

She pushed her way to the table, studied the red
book and returned to claim her purse. "Something, something, *General Techniques of Hypnotism,*" she told him.

"Why not, George?"

"You've got to be kidding, Louise!" he objected. "Hypnosis? Me? Not in a pink fit! Not in a million years, girl. Hypnosis scares me. And, jeez, I can't spare any more time, Lou Lou."

"Suit yourself," she told him. "I think you'd be good at it."

"Sure, sure," he told her.

Louise managed to procure almost all the books she wanted. Three days without food, her calculations told her, but she promised him they would not be three days in a row. Her dedication to her studies bordered on obsession.

"This is plain bloody ridiculous," he told her gruffly as he carried half of her books towards his car. He had no other words for it. "Why does one of my best friends have to be an idiot?" he asked her. "Try for a small increase in your allowance, girl."

George worried about her. She was still growing at that time, but her parents were very poor.

Hard work is what made Louise an ace full-time student. She had barely scraped in with her university entrance exam. She deserved a ride home to her shared flat, with all those heavy books to transport, George felt, and also to save her the bus fare home. She often walked two miles to save a little of her meager allowance, and she was one of the few who never smoked any cigarettes. Louise Hewitt really deserved a whole lot more than an occasional ride home. She was a trooper.

"You, yourself must be the cause of it, George," she suddenly suggested.

"Of what?" Barnard was concentrating on the traffic.

"That red chocolate box you get shoved under your

nose every time," she laughed. "When did it start?"

"Months ago."

"Did you have anything in particular on your mind?" she inquired. She was watching him closely.

Barnard needed to think. Then he remembered what it was, but he hesitated. He felt somewhat uncomfortable about sharing his thoughts.

"I can see on your face that you know what it was, George," she asserted.

"I healed somebody. It's long ago," he answered. "It was weird. And now it has come back to haunt me . . . sort of. Forget about it."

There was a lengthy silence. They had reached Louise's flat, but the young woman refused to hop out of his car. "Tell me what happened," she bluntly insisted.

"A friend of mine was seriously ill. I sat there, holding her head, and I felt a mass of energy leave my body. She was healed. But later that day, I threw a whopper of a fit. A panic attack or an epileptic fit. Perhaps it was a panic attack that turned into an epileptic fit. Who knows? It scared the daylights out of me at the time. But she was healed. She stopped bleeding, finally, instantly, months and months after she gave birth." Barnard paused.

"Strangely, two people told me I would become a healer. They told me that shortly before this thing actually happened. That's what's been on my mind lately, and I've asked myself the question, 'Where do I go from here?' And then I decided the Spirits could sort it out on my behalf. They know I'm busy."

"You should have at least put in your bid on that book," Louise suggested. "It went for just two dollars, you know. Now you'll have to pay for a brand new one."

"Give it a break, Lou Lou," he told her. "And don't

forget to write your name in all those books, you dreamer." He helped her unload her newly purchased treasures.

"Bloody hypnosis!" he grunted. "I'm spread too thin as it is, Louise."

There was to be no break in George's 11:11 wake-up calls. No break, either, in the dreams that showed him that unusual red "chocolate box."

Perhaps Louise picked it right, he thought. She's super-intuitive.

He reassessed his duties and commitments, and delegated some responsibilities. His activities were now streamlined to the point where, if needed, he could take on extra studies besides the twice-weekly lectures in industrial psychology. Months had gone by since the auction. Neither Louise Hewitt nor George Barnard made further comments on that unusual healing of Janelle Gillies, the box of chocolates, or the red book.

A group of female first-year psychology students were seated on the psychology department's lawn. There was a lot of chitchat, occasional whispering, giggling, and laughter. Louise and George were just leaving one of the nearby lecture theaters when he heard a voice in his right ear.

"They are talking about what you need to know." Undeniably, this was the voice of a male Spirit Guardian, for there was no one to be seen.

He grabbed Louise by the shoulder. "Those girls over there are talking about my next project, Louise," he told her. "I was advised about that just now. It's still jolly well ringing in my ear."

"Let's find out what it is," she told him.

"No," he answered her. "You do it. Go check it out." He sensed the girls might clam up with him around. They would, however, freely confide in Louise.

She dropped her books and joined the group while he waited. When she came back, she was grinning from ear to ear. "Clinical hypnotherapy," she said, "that's what they're on about. Two of them are doing that deal. Don't tell me I didn't say so, George." She handed him a leaflet with all the details of the course.

"You're sharp, Lou Lou," he told her. "You're worth your weight in nickels."

"I'm positively brilliant at times," she answered. "I truly amaze myself. And I won't hurt your feelings by telling you each lecture day that I damned well told you so."

"Bloody hell," he swore. "I don't think I'm going to like this hypnosis thing." He knew the Spirit Guardian's suggestion was the nearest thing to a direct order. At least, it felt that way.

~

It was a small, privately owned company in town that taught the nuts-and-bolts aspects of hypnosis. Sadly, the university was doing very little in this somewhat controversial field. George agonized about it for a few more months, then he booked in over the telephone and sent them his check. Their recommended book list was enormous, but he ordered all the books. A huge box full of reading materials and manuals soon arrived. That bright red book, a copy of the one Louise had wanted him to bid on, was on top of the stack in that box. "Gawd!"

But time and again, George failed the final exam on some pretext or other. He had arrived at the school with a bad attitude about hypnosis, and it was obvious to all. He could have bought that little company a few times over without upsetting his bank balance too much, and the proprietors knew it. He questioned every method, every approach, and they hated him for it.

George Mathieu Barnard was not popular in that private school. For reasons he did not yet understand, they feared him. He was good at doing the very thing he had never wanted to know about, whilst breaking all their "rules." The experience with Janelle Gillies had taught him that he could reach out, touch his patients on the forehead, and the healing would begin. Quickly. Right then. From that very moment on.

But being knocked back, over and over again, for the diploma he felt he richly deserved bothered him endlessly.

When he announced he would begin to teach others the art of hypnosis, his old school quickly invited him to sit for yet another exam. Barnard's devious plot had worked. The massive sum of money he claimed to have allocated for his new school of learning frightened them. But if George succeeded in his plan, they could always claim that they were his teachers, first and foremost.

It was perverse, underhanded, and dishonest of Barnard—he admits it—and he loved every aspect of that bogus plan. The usual charge for the exam would be waived, he was told. Wow! That should really interest poor little George Mathieu! Naturally, he passed with flying colors. He got a certificate that looked like a million dollars, had it framed, and promptly forgot about it.

He found it a week later by the side of the homestead. "Oh? Cripes! Oh, yes! I wondered where I left the stupid thing!"

It was wrecked by two days of gentle rain, bleached by five days of intense sunshine—a crinkled mess of hard-to-read pulp. He keeps it on file for a laugh. Gaining it meant nothing, but it stopped a lot of sniping and it also brought him much respect in his new profession.

He deserved respect for his many successes in his newfound occupation and the visualization techniques he developed. He did not appreciate the kind of respect that was born out of needless fear.

Two years went by, and he gradually built up his clientele. Out of the more than twenty local general practitioners, counselors, and specialists he had canvassed, most were too overworked, too busy, or too uninterested to see him. Just two doctors were now sending him the occasional patient. But ex-patients were recommending others to go and see Barnard.

The treatment of a preponderance of potential suicide victims, as well as likely "reoffenders" who had failed to cash in on that last ticket to nowhere, would finally bring George Mathieu face to face with the Spirit Guardians. It would only be in retrospect that he would realize how the Spirit Guardians provided him for many years with a fair percentage of their emergencies.

The Guardians also played their part in the unlikely-to-succeed task of turning the owner of a repetition manufacturing plant into a healer. They needed to get involved. Of his own accord, the young businessman was not inclined to make a move in that direction. Yet, he was a natural at the work, and if there is such a thing as fate, here was an instance where fate needed a little bit of a shove in the right direction.

The Spirit Guardians still remained elusive, as week after week, year after year, George Mathieu received his 11:11 wake-up calls, instantly going back to sleep and again waking in the mornings, frequently already knowing not only who he would be treating but what he would be treating this patient for.

Remember the little girl picking the petals from the daisies? Imagine her sitting there a whole week long, saying, "He woves me. . . he woves me not. . . he woves me. . ." Seven days. Seven nights.

Even before the girl started her self-appointed task, Eternity already knew how many white petals she would pull from the golden flower heads, how many would drift onto the waters of the canal, how many would remain on the bank. Eternity would know all this, even before she was born, for Eternity spans all of time and Eternity can foresee.

But in no way would this predetermine anything in the time/space existence of the child. This three-year-old sprite was endowed with a free will—then, as she is now. She could choose to

denude fifty flowers, one hundred, or many more.
Her choice entirely. She could change her fickle
little mind a thousand times. Yet, in Eternity her
every move, her every word, was already known.

For Spirit Guardians, sandwiched somewhere between Eternity and our "real," human
time, this presents a problem. In the case of a
calamity in the making, they may perhaps at times
intervene and thwart someone's free will. To play
fortune teller to another would not be in their
charter. It would amount to gross interference
with mortal free will.

No one had suggested that George become
a manufacturer. It was the young migrant's idea
entirely. He had taken charge of his life, arguably
because he was too dumb to know he couldn't do
it. Too naive to believe he could ever fail. Too
optimistic to foresee the pitfalls. But he had indeed
taken charge. And it could have been his decision
to do anything with his free will . . . even pluck
petals from daisies.

In retrospect, and at a crucial crossroads in
his life, he had thrown his future into the laps of
the Spirit Guardians he well knew existed, for
them to decide what was to happen next.

He had robbed himself of his free-will
prerogatives, leaving the Spirit Guardians with the
responsibility of deciding what next would happen in his life. Neither did he spell out his need to
be guided, nor did he realize he had failed to do
so.

The Guardians would surely have needed
to break all rules of ethical conduct if they had told
him precisely what to do. Showing him that bright
red "chocolate box book" and, finally, telling him

what he needed to know, not what he needed to do, was perhaps as far as they could go.

With a crystal-clear eternal blueprint of his future in their minds, and irrational fears of both hypnosis and potential resulting fits in Barnard's mind, there was still no one with the license to dictate, or even suggest, George Mathieu's next move.

For many months, George's complete unawareness of having overlooked these not-negotiable mortal free-will prerogatives had slowed his progress. Some clever engineering by the Guides had created the seeming coincidences that put Barnard back on track.

The Guides never gave up on him.

Their presence would soon become much more obvious.

Will It All Make Sense?

Even now, opinions remain divided.
Are our universes exploding, moving ever outward into
    deep space? Or are we simply confused in our
    observations and calculations by the inexplicably
    diverse movements of millions of galaxies that will all
    . . . eventually . . . find their own stable orbit?

Science says maybe. Faith says they will.
The ultimate proof of a highly organized, friendly,
    mutually beneficial Alliance of Perfectly Balanced
Universes may be a billion millennia away.
There surely are some intriguing indications
    it may come about.

So far, the age-old trajectories of Earth and her sister
    planets, at least, appear to happily point at total
    equilibrium being a major objective of the Great
Master's plan. How nice to know, reassuring.

But the occasional fragments of a definitive answer
    will only come to those who stubbornly keep
    asking the pertinent questions.

And in this segment of the documentation we again
    move back in time, observing some psychic events,
    inexplicable healings—some may call them miracles
    and stubbornly re-ask the questions in order to
    discover more about the Spirit Guardians,
    the owners of the voices that have guided
    so many on this planet . . .
    . . . and for it all to make sense.

part four

Inexplicable Healings

Doctor Hugh Byrnes was one of the two general practitioners who on occasion referred patients to Barnard's clinic. He was tall, young— perhaps only about thirty years old when they first met—loud, quite rude, and somewhat manic for a medical man.

Noticeably, and on the frequent occasions Barnard visited his clinic, there appeared to always be a majority of females in his waiting rooms. The women seemed to like his somewhat unrefined jokes and easygoing, boyish ways. He was, however, said to be a clever, intuitive diagnostician.

"I'm not going to let you loose on my patients," the doctor told George bluntly, "but I've got enough problems of my own I wouldn't bother tell you about. I suggest you teach me how to hypnotize myself. And if you're any bloody good, I'll solve my own problems with the use of what you can teach me. After that, you can count on my sending you as many of my patients as require your attention."

And so it was agreed.

Early on, the doctor learned to self-hypnotize under Barnard's guidance. Surprisingly for one so unbelieving, discerning, even critical, he was brilliant at it. Their work together on the self-hypnosis project cemented a kind of friendship, certainly great respect, between the two men. Yet, some elusive element of competition would always remain between the GP and the hyp-notherapist.

One of the patients Dr. Byrnes referred to Barnard experienced a most marvelous healing. Unforgettable.

It would never be duplicated in more than thirty years.

9

Sweet Old Alice

Prospectors looking for gold have a saying. It goes something like this: If you think you've found color in your pan, you haven't. But if you really do strike gold, you *know.*

George Mathieu has been a prospector for many years, looking for spiritual gems and psychic gold, and he has a saying of his own. It goes like this: Let it happen and flow with the tide, expect the outrageous, and don't analyze the workings of it. Above all, stay relaxed. That's his saying, and he stands by it.

Well . . . mostly, he does. There are times when those spiritual gems scare the living daylights out of him and he becomes far from relaxed. Neurotic even.

So it was with Alice.

Doctor Hugh Byrnes warned him about the patient he was referring for an urgent evening hypnotherapy session. He had christened her "That five foot and four inches of unstoppable eighty-two-year-old bulldozer."

Her real name was Alice, and she would be ruthless in attack and surely take Barnard's clinic by storm. Blood would flow in copious amounts, the doctor predicted. The only good thing about her, he claimed, was that she could not be insulted, ever.

Hugh Byrnes was right, as always.

She dapperly marched up the clinic path towards George, who was waiting to greet her beneath the clinic lights. She almost shouted at him, "You've got no beard!" It sounded like an accusation. "The other fellow had a beard! A black beard."

"Well, jolly good for *him!*" He let her have it. "Mine's blond and gray, and I scrape it off whenever people more considerate than you are permit me the time." He was ready to give her a lot more cheek, but she moved into the arc of the lights and left him speechless. She was suffering from the worst attack of psoriasis he had ever seen.

She slipped past him and stood by the recliner chair, saying, "I suppose I sit here?" Not waiting for an answer, she dropped her generous purse to the floor and lowered her less than one hundred pounds into the recliner. "I don't tell people my age," she informed him, "so don't be so rude as to ask. And I've been hypnotized before. I know all about it. One session is all I need, and I want a pensioner discount. I state my case; no good beating about the bush."

"You've managed to really tick me off," he told her. "A record under-two minutes is all it took for you to do that." He kicked the door shut, turned on his heel, and closed in on the tough little old bat. "I'm a hundred years old, lady, two hundred maybe," he told her. "I'm an angry old man who's had a rotten, tiring day. You look about forty, fifty at the most. You get no pensioner discount, and I don't need a black beard to hypnotize you. You're easy!"

She giggled sweetly and said in a most charming little voice, "Master Barnard . . . I had to know if you had the oomph to do a good job on me. It's all in my mind, so you can take it all out of my mind. In one session." She added pleadingly, meekly, childlike, "I'm not very well off."

"You're all flipping bark and no bite, Alice," he grumbled at her. He pulled up a chair and studied her psoriasis-ravaged face and open sores. "Jeez, you look a mess, girl. What brought this on? And who's the fellow with the black beard?"

"Dubois," she answered. "I went looking for him, but he passed away. Victor Dubois, with his black beard and his watch. He came from France as well, you know."

"Close, Alice. He actually was a Belgian," George contradicted her statement.

"Yes, that too. Same thing. From all the way over there, like you," she agreed.

"Yes, but Victor turned people into chickens and rabbits and monkeys. He didn't do any clinical work, did he?" George asked. "Old Victor loved the stage."

"Master Dubois fixed me up just like that with his black beard and his watch." She cleverly moved her eyes from left to right and back again as if they were following a swinging watch. "And you can do it, too," she reassured George. "I can tell. I'm not as dumb as the average old tart. I know you can. Look at my legs." She poked out her badly marked little legs. "Look at my chest!" She started to undo her dress.

"Keep your shirt on, Alice. For heaven's sake! I'm bashful with the, uh, more mature woman." Her giggling told him he'd been tricked. She never intended to bare her chest. "You are a holy terror, girl. Now, will you tell me what brought this on?"

"Darcie died. Darcie was my husband. He was a good man, my Darcie. A boiler blew up at his work and they never found most of him."

Her sad eyes focused on his frowning face. "George . . . can I call you George?" And since he nodded she could, she carried on confidently, "George, that left me with thirteen kids to care for and the fourteenth on the way." She needed to pause, and all of her being momentarily reflected the indescribable trauma of long ago.

Soon she proceeded with her tale of woe. "Well, the next day I felt itchy all over, and the day after that, I looked like this. And nothing the doctors could give me would help. Then the neighbors took me to see Master Dubois, after his show was over. Victor Dubois, with his black beard and his watch, and he told me I couldn't have all those sores with so many children to care for. So, guess what? They went away!"

"You puzzle me," George told her. "I don't get it, Alice. That was then, this is now. You still haven't told me what brought this on."

"Last week Benjamin got married. He's my youngest. He's out there waiting for me in the car. He'll be forty-one next June and he married this lovely lass who has two children already. Just like that, I've got thirty-one grandchildren instead of twenty-nine.

"Jeez, don't you get it? No more kids, and now this has come back."

He laughed. "You cooked and washed and cleaned . . . for Benjamin? All this time? Woman, you show an insight . . . well, never mind." He was enjoying her immensely. "Didn't anyone inform you that you should be quite senile by now? You can never trust those government departments. What a public service over-sight. But you're still streetwise on everything, I bet. Lie back in that chair, Alice. I promise you a heavy session you'll never forget."

She seemed delighted with his comments and stretched out her little body.

"A thousand years from now, Alice," he told her, "in heaven. No! Wait! For you and me, the other place, most likely. You'll hear my voice and you'll say, 'There goes George Barnard. He gave me no pensioner discount, but he did a crackerjack job on me. He's got the oomph, and I would recognize his voice anywhere.'"

He took a brooch with imitation emerald from his desk drawer and held it up for her to see. "Take a deep breath, Alice. Concentrate on this beautiful stone. . ."

"Your watch, young man!" she yelled at him.

"I beg your pardon?"

"You can't hypnotize me without a watch! Are you a fake?"

"After years of study," he lied, "the magic is now in the stone."

"Jeepers! That must have been difficult for you."

"It was! Sheer agony. Now concentrate. Sleepy-byes for you, Alice. . ."

Hypnotic induction was followed by a deepening of the trance. Then some ego strengthening before he deep-ened the trance even more by slowly turning the dimmer for the clinic lights. Each time he barefooted his way past the switch, he turned the dial the tiniest of fractions. Finally he triggered self-hypnosis to more accurately touch his patient's therapy needs.

He suddenly felt guided. Surrounded by Spirit Helpers. Hit it, Barnard, he thought. You're on a roll.

The English phrases, accented by the singsong drawl of his ancient foreign dialect, would forever remain locked in her mind.

Victor Dubois's therapy had been powerful indeed, but it had been subject to her caring for her off-spring. With Benjamin's departure from the parental home, well over forty years of Victor's post-hypnotic suggestions had suddenly reached their use-by date. Barnard's therapy would need to last her for the remainder of her life. It had better last. This sprightly old thing might still live twenty years, even more. Anyone's guess.

He cast his eyes towards the ceiling and prayed: Help me with this, you Guys, for you may never find one more deserving than this precious child of the Gods.

In the near darkness of the clinic, the diminutive form of his patient appeared lost in the big reclining chair. He strained his eyes to make out her features, but to no avail.

Time passed, and it appeared she had shrunk even more. She might eventually dissolve into the fabric of her chair, leaving only a radiant, glowing outline where her body had been. She—body, Spirit, and soul—might soon be ascending to another realm.

He carried on. *But is it I choosing these words?* His eyes were hurting. A visual disturbance? Another epileptic fit? Fearful memories of long ago flooded back into his mind. Please? Please, not now. Please, no more fits, he begged.

The outline of his patient's body gradually became brighter and brighter. He continued to pace the floor, but questioned who was selecting the phrases for the old girl's therapy. If they were his words, he surely wasn't thinking about what he was saying. It had happened so many times before. It was happening again. Alice, you are listening to the words of love of an Entity much greater than I am, said his mind. You have found grace in the eyes of your Creator. With these words, heal thyself, Old Dear.

The clinic timepiece indicated that almost two hours had flown by. Could that be right? he wondered almost out loud. He aided his patient in the routine of surfacing from the trance, and slowly turned the lights back up. Then he stood as if nailed to the floor. He hardly recognized the woman. He had never witnessed anyone heal so fast.

"Cat's got your tongue now?" she giggled. "You waffled on for ever and a long weekend, Sonny. I'll pay you now. I'm going. I'm not coming back. One session is all I can afford, like I said."

"Stay there!" he growled at her. He handed her a small mirror and she inspected her face.

"Yes, that's the old me," she said. Then, looking up, "Oh, those few scaly bits? They'll be gone by morning. They'll rub off on my pillow." She hopped from the recliner and reached for her purse. "Time to settle my debts," she said.

"I don't charge for miracles," he told her. "Go home, woman. And for goodness' sake, be kind to Benjamin." He held out the brooch. "Wear this magic brooch once a week. No more psoriasis, ever."

She hesitated, then stepped back. Overawed by his

offering her the most important tool of his trade, she point-blank refused to even touch it.

"Do as you're told, you dumb old bat," he told her with a smile. He knew it was the required bedside manner to get her to take it.

She accepted the brooch with both hands, dropped it into her purse, and gave him a hug. He watched her, awestruck, as she happily scampered down the path to where Benjamin was waiting in the car.

He needed to make a strong coffee. Quickly. He needed a cigarette. Urgently! He needed to think. "Christ, You scared twelve months of growth out of me," he mumbled at the unseen Master of the Universe. Jesus, he thought, I was sure I was going to have to hand her back to Benjamin all swept up in a dustpan. "God! You must have a sense of the ludicrous. I was sure You'd switched patients on me in the dark."

He nervously puffed away at his cigarette and poured and sipped at the piping-hot brew. "Don't mind me," he suggested. "You freaked me out! I thought I was going to chuck another fit."

He felt himself relax once more and continued the one-way conversation like a child who knows it has been tricked by an older sibling, "You sent me a yogi! For sure, You did! She would have light bulbs for breakfast, that one. She chews away at engine parts for lunch. Sleeps on a bed of nails, I shouldn't wonder." He laughed at the thought. "Thank You for that precious experience."

Mischievously, and for the benefit of the ever-present Seraphim, he added, "Do me a favor, please, sweethearts. Chalk up that discussion on the credit side of my ledger. Call it a prayer. You know how busy I get." He felt sure they would oblige.

Seraphim will do almost anything for you.

⁓

"I saw sweet Alice this morning, George." Hugh Byrnes sounded excited, bewildered, and still doubtful of what he had witnessed. All of these feelings were evident in the tone of the doctor's voice. "Not a mark on her! Not a blemish! What did you do to her?"

"Nothing," Barnard answered. "Nothing much. But I did give her an extra long session, that's for sure. Nearly two whole hours."

"Bloody fantastic!" came the shout down the line. Hugh Byrnes would never learn to mince his words. "What was she like when she left your clinic last night?" he asked.

"Almost healed," George suggested. "There was some loose skin, like . . . flaky bits. Otherwise, she was fine. No more open sores that I could see."

It was silent on the other end of the line. Dr. Byrnes always tended to hang up abruptly, mostly without a good-bye, but George knew he was still there. "I see it, but I don't believe it," the medico remarked. "I'm not ever again going to fool around with psoriasis. They're all yours. You make me look bad, Barnard."

"Sorry, but it's got nothing to do with me." George was quickly on the defensive. "Don't ever expect it to go as fast as that again."

"How's that?"

"It's her," he answered. "Her mind. Her level of

expectation. Her ability to concentrate, relax, visualize. Didn't she tell you she smashes a dozen beer bottles in her bath before she hops in? Didn't you know she opens spaghetti cans with her teeth? The woman's a yogi, Hugh. I just did what I always do. Why don't you take a few minutes and really get to know your more talented patients? You work too hard."

"You bullshit too much," came the swift response. "Eh! Eh! George! Alice let me feel the magic in that fake ten-cent emerald. Boy, you can lay it on thick. It's an art form with you. Why doesn't that ever work for me?" The line went dead.

"Again! I hate it when he does that," the therapist growled.

The Light, the Golden Glow, as George Mathieu calls it, is a wonder to behold. He was privileged to witness the phenomenon on a number of occasions in his clinic and elsewhere. He regards it to be a spiritual rescue package for those who are deeply troubled and suicidal. All these at-risk individuals were aged between thirty and forty, with a mean age of thirty-four.

But this was not the case with Alice. She was fine, psychologically speaking. To this day, her experience remains the only occasion of this kind when the physical, not the mental, healing process was so greatly accelerated. What makes her instance more remarkable is that it happened to her at the advanced age of eighty-two.

It's Barnard's theory—theory only and nothing more—that the partial lack of synchronization of the human mind with the Spiritual Powers at work was, and remains, the cause of his discomfort at those times. He suffered from headaches, blurred or double vision, severe eyestrain and, on one of those occasions, partial blindness.

And he still wouldn't have missed it for the world.

Events such as these instilled in him the desire to get to know the Spiritual Beings who so ably assisted in making these healings come about.

10

The Survivor

Little Christopher Sutton was born with a huge, dark birthmark on his belly. In the shape of a man's hand and almost that size, it made the mother's story about the mark almost believable.

Emily claimed that on hearing the news of his son's birth fully a week before he was expected, her husband had raced over from his engineering works without first washing his hands. Brian Sutton, it was alleged, had put his professional stamp on their freshly born infant, and the handprint would never wash off. Christopher was now destined to become an engineer. Probably a hydraulics engineer, she professed.

There was merit in that grand assumption. The little chap always loved his bath and was unafraid of water. Emily often brought him around on hot days, and the Barnards would take turns playing with the toddler in their pool. Nothing delighted little Christopher more than being splashed all over. He would chuckle and squeal with excitement.

Seated on the swimming pool steps, the water baby safely between them, the mother and George Mathieu were taking turns pouring water from a plastic bucket over the boy's head. Everyone else was lazing around in the pool.

"He'll be sporting gills and fins soon," George warned Emily, "and scales all over. And he'll want to sleep in your bathtub at night. I've seen it happen before—suddenly, overnight, on their second birthday precisely. He'll frighten the milkman out of his wits. No more milk deliveries for you."

"Still almost two months to go," she laughed. "Too far off to worry about it now."

The discussion, it seemed, was going right over little Christopher's head, together with the buckets of water. They were keeping it coming, but now at irregular intervals, watching him screw up his little face in the excitement of anticipation of the next sudden wave to hit him from above.

"His special trademark is fading rather rapidly," George remarked to Emily. It had become hard to discern. It was almost gone. But George had spoken softly, thinking the little fellow might have become self-conscious about the mark on his belly.

Emily had no time to answer Barnard. The little one looked up at George, saying, "A spear did that. It killed me." His facial expression was deadly serious. He was stating a cold, hard fact!

"Did you hear that?" Emily asked. Then she changed her mind. "Did I dream that or did I actually hear it?" she wanted to know from everyone around.

Everyone in the pool had heard it—six others, adults and children both. They were all staring at the little man in shocked disbelief. He had spoken so clearly. His words had almost sounded prophetic. They all agreed he had truly said it.

George was stunned and didn't know what to say.

"That's by far the most words he's ever strung together," the mother claimed.

"You should have seen his face," George told her. "I never saw such a serious expression on a pair of puffy cheeks."

"More!" said Christopher. He meant for them to keep the buckets coming. He had jolly well waited long enough. His precious pool time was being wasted.

Hours later, he had no recollection of having said the words he had so clearly spoken. At a little under two years of age, would he know what a spear was? What being killed could mean? Why had he addressed George Mathieu? Why not Emily? That little nipper puzzled Barnard.

As Christopher lay on his left side on his little bath towel, next to his mom, the fingers of that fading "handprint" looked like ancient blood streaming down. The specter of reincarnation was haunting George again. As always, he would put it right back in the too-hard basket. The concept bothered him.

He had met too many reincarnated Cleopatras.

The Australian coral reefs George knew so well were amongst the most fascinating in the world. But he could never see them all, or anywhere near enough of them. The lure of the reefs was in his blood, but reefs can harbor danger. He was looking for a dive partner in Sanur, on the island of Bali. He soon found one—a young American mother who lived there almost permanently. She was in the import/export business, but had time on her hands and any number of baby-sitters at a moment's notice. She also knew the best diving spots.

They were soon on their way to the beach in the steaming mid-morning heat.

George pointed to one of a number of European-style homes in a street of mostly Balinese kampongs. "It looks like it has been transported whole, from my home town and halfway around the globe, without breaking into bits," George told her. "Clever!"

There was a mischievous smile on her face as she steered him towards its front door. "We'll tell them what you said," she suggested, "and ask them for a cup of tea."

"You've got to be kidding, Jenny," he told her, as she brazenly rang the doorbell and made as if she would quickly run away.

Barnard was wondering what sort of a cheeky imp he had scored for a dive buddy.

"My American girlfriend lives here, George," she said. "She's in the export business, just like my family."

That information made him feel good about waiting for a total stranger to answer the door. The air conditioning in the home would make him feel even better. They were welcomed by a tall, cheerful young woman who was pleased to see them both. Her little boy of just eighteen months did not appear to share her feelings. He placed himself on the floor in front of George and stared at him with deep-sunken, dark-ringed, forbidding eyes. Practically without blinking, this little chap was studying Barnard intently. It looked as though a smile would never make the mistake of crossing his lips. This was a wise old little man who was psyching out the analyst.

The mother had noticed his behavior and sensed her visitor to be uncomfortable with the pushy little guy's behavior. No child had ever reacted to George in that strange way. He was staring at the man with impudence and a strange determination George had never seen before. What does he want to know from me? Barnard wondered.

"Leave the man alone, Ricky!" the mother warned whilst stamping her foot. She turned to her visitor. "He's never done that before, George." Turning next to Jenny, she asked, "Has he now?"

The child ignored her and kept looking at George as if the man had stolen the very last of his favorite sticky candy bars, making the therapist wonder what was going on in that little mind.

"He's always so well behaved, Lisah," Jenny remarked. "George, this is so unusual for him, honest it is."

"Does he have a father?" Barnard jokingly asked. "He's looking at me as if he's never seen a white male in his life."

His comment evoked some laughter and the quick assurance that Ricky did indeed have a father, who had only just left for the market. The laughter was short lived. The mother had had enough of the child's weird behavior. She called out loudly, "Putu!"

A Balinese caretaker around ten years of age came running, and it was clear this young man was to scoop up the child and take him away. But Ricky would have none of it. He screamed a strange throaty yell, slid along the floor towards George, and kept staring up at him. The little caretaker stood there studying George and the whole scene. Slowly, wide-eyed and full of fear, the young native child backed himself into a corner of the room. In the next moment he was gone.

"Would you believe that?" Jenny asked. She turned to Barnard and explained, "They are really beautiful people here in Bali. Nothing pleases them more than to please you. But Putu is frightened of what's going on. He is superstitious, that's all, and he wasn't looking at you, George. He was looking at someone next to you. He probably thought he saw a Spirit."

"He always does what I ask him to do," Lisah suggested angrily, ignoring Jenny's remarks. "This is the first time ever he's refused."

The little fellow on the floor was getting up. He was moving in on George, crowding him, almost threateningly. Then, suddenly, his arms came forward and he showed George his inner arms. They were full of weeping sores. The child had George practically pinned down with his relentless stare.

"Ricky!" the mother warned him in a shrill voice. She was really distressed now, but George wondered why she stamped her foot on the floor each time she yelled at the child.

"Leave him, please, Lisah," Barnard told her. "He knows I know what's wrong with him. If I can cool down my overheated brain, I'll think of it."

"What are you?" she asked.

"It is terminal," said a loud voice. As always, no one else had heard it.

Instantly, George rebelled, angrily. Doesn't damned well look like it. His mind had ever so quickly formulated that response.

"It is terminal," came the message once again.

"Jeez," he muttered under his breath.

"Some sort of healer, Lisah," he finally answered the mother. He was racking his brains trying to think of what he had learned, and where. There were so many of those dumb courses in the last twelve years, too many. My brains are numb with physiology, psychology, neurology, and psychopharmacology . . . and the rest of those flaming "ologies," he thought.

Finally, he had to give up. He and Jenny were leaving for the reef, and little Ricky followed him all the way to the door, robot-like, his little arms still in front of him. Barnard lovingly touched him on his snowy white mop-top and told him he was sorry, but he could not remember.

"She's had him with the doctors for months," Jenny informed him. "They can't figure out what's wrong with the boy. I suppose he'll grow out of it. He is a survivor."

Barnard knew the child would not survive. He was critical.

If this information passed on by the Guides was incorrect, Barnard decided, it would be the first bum steer ever. Whoever owned the voice had told no lies in all those years.

The reef was exquisitely beautiful, but George had an exquisitely troublesome time. He couldn't get the little chap out of his mind. Finally, on the way back, he could stand it no longer.

"We have to call in on Ricky and Lisah," he told his dive buddy. "I have to find out what's wrong with him. I must remember."

"We're on the wrong street," Jenny answered. She stopped to point out, "It's over there, running parallel to this one."

"We have to go back there then," he told her.

"It's so-o-o hot," she argued.

Just then, Ricky came running around the corner,

right up to them, and out came his little arms again, urgently this time. That brutally piercing stare was again aimed at George Mathieu. Some fifty paces behind him, the desperate caretaker, Putu, came running after the child he was responsible for. Another fifty paces behind the young Balinese came the out-of-breath but somewhat relieved mother. But Jenny's shocked face said it all. This small child was not allowed to be on the busy streets; not even with his youthful caretaker was he allowed out. Ricky had somehow sensed their return and slipped out of Putu's clutches.

"What are you?" the mother was shouting at George. She was shaking like a leaf, moving between them to protect her child.

The bloody Pied Piper, about to steal your kid, he was thinking. "Some sort of healer," he told her once again, but bluntly. He took the boy by the hand. "Come on, little man," he told him. "We'll find out what is wrong with you if it takes all day. All day today, and tomorrow as well, I promise."

~

"What is he being treated for, Lisah?" Barnard asked.

"They don't know what's wrong with him," she answered. She found a tube of cream and handed it to George. It was just a common antibiotic. "It doesn't work. The fluid and dirt keeps weeping up from under the cream. Only the edges heal."

There was a clue! But George missed it completely. His mind had also gone on holiday, it seemed—but elsewhere, not in Bali. He thoroughly checked the child's long hair for ticks. Nothing there. And Ricky just stood there, patiently, arms out, his eyes on the therapist's. Somehow George no longer felt ill at ease with him. Here was a smart little kid, who knew what was in George's mind and understood the many long years of study that was behind him. It now felt good to be with him. If only. . .

"An allergy?" George was thinking out loud. "From the soil?"

"All the kampong kids from next door come and dig in our yard," Lisah argued. "They're not allowed to in their yard; it's full of rice now, so they come here. They're all okay."

"Poison, in the house. Show me where he sleeps," Barnard suggested. But Ricky's room was freshly painted with an acrylic. His raw timber cot had no lead paint on it. The bedding was spotless, the mosquito net brand-new. Yet, George felt he was now on the trail.

Ricky hadn't moved. He was still standing there in front of George's empty chair, his little arms still up and in front of him. There was nothing left to check but his food. Then, suddenly, the therapist received the needed electrochemical burst to his gray matter. The spark he had been waiting for. Oriental medicine! It was so long ago. He counted the sores on the boy's arms—twenty-one on his right arm, only eighteen lesser sores on his left arm. His little legs were similarly affected.

"There's something in his food that's slowly doing him in, Lisah," he told the mother.

That statement upset the mother. Suddenly she came alive. "He eats what the natives eat!" she growled at the man. "None of *them* ever gets sick!" Lisah was thoroughly riled.

"Something extra," George insisted.

The two women looked at each other. Barnard had struck gold. He knew it, sensed it. This was it. The problem was solved, but what was it?

"Two eggs a day," the mother finally mumbled. "The biggest double yolkers I can buy."

"What else, Lisah?" The therapist was pressing the point.

"And a liter of milk, most days more," she admitted. "And straight from the farm."

"Protein poisoning," he told her.

"It is so," came the clearly audible reply out of nowhere.

Ricky instantly lost interest in him. He toddled off. He knew it, too, and never gave George a second's glance from that moment on.

"I never saw it before, Lisah," George admitted to the mother. "I learned about it years ago, and I forgot about it. Not everyone reacts like he does. Few do, actually. Cut out the extras. He'll be fine."

They had trudged almost halfway back to the hotel in the searing heat. His mind was still with the little man with the snowy, mop-top hairdo. "Funny little chap, isn't he?" Barnard remarked. "Do you realize, Jenny, the little guy never said a single word to me?"

She stopped him in the middle of the street, holding him by the shoulder. She was laughing in his face and gyrating about. She needed to hold on to him for support or she would have been lying on the pavement with those laughing fits. She was causing a mighty stir. People were stopping to see what these two weird foreigners were all about.

Finally, she hit a patch of urgently needed rationality. "Oh, my God!" she shouted. "He's deaf and dumb! Ricky's deaf and dumb! Jeez! How slow are you?" Then she started to laugh all over again. She wouldn't walk on. "That's why Lisah stamps on the floor! So Ricky can feel the vibrations! God!" She started to wobble all over again with laughter.

For a moment, he seriously considered taking her hands off him and leaving her there. Some Balinese folks had grouped themselves around the pair, and they were laughing as well. The natives had not a clue about what was going on, but it seemed not to matter to them. Jenny was the spectacle. Then she got the hiccups, a violent bout of them, and she blamed him for her distress.

"Jenny," he told her later, "I mentioned protein poisoning, and Ricky instantly knew. He wandered off immediately—the moment I said it. How deaf can he be?"

She frowned at him. "Stone deaf! So, what? This is Bali, George. Things happen. Get used to it. The place is loaded with Spirits that tell you things."

She was deadly serious. Barnard knew better than to speak up about the voices he had heard all his life. As a student of psychology, he always still remained touchy about publicly owning up to his witnessing the phenomenon.

He wanted to know how the little man was faring; the Barnard family would be leaving for home the following day. But the walk was too far for George in that day's steaming heat. He decided to check with Jenny.

"I saw him yesterday," she informed him. "All his sores are healed. His scars are almost gone, too," she added. "The boy is now very lively again."

He told her he was pleased, and would she say hello to Lisah and Ricky when she saw them next.

"Of course," she told him. Then she surprised him by saying, "You owed him."

"Owed who?" he asked, thinking he hadn't heard her correctly.

"You owed Ricky," she insisted. "Who knows what you did to him in another life?"

"Jenny? For God's sake!" he grunted at her. "I chose to be a therapist. I didn't choose to live this life to pay outstanding debts."

"Why did you come to Bali?" she asked.

"To give my wife and children a holiday," he answered.

"You left them all in the hotel pool, George, on that day. You went off to our reef, but actually you went to pay a debt. You even took me along to make sure you could find your creditor. You owed a debt, Ricky collected, and he owes you nothing. He knew, and he instantly turned away from you when you found out what was wrong with him. He still hasn't forgiven you for what you did to him in another life."

"One and one make two," George told her, "every time. But an almost infinite number of fractions can make up the total of that sum, Jenny. How can you look at the effect of a healing today and determine its causes in previous existences? It would depress the daylights out of me if I believed this universe to be continuously in the red with all of us constantly repaying old debts."

"So, why did you become a healer?" she asked.

"To accumulate spiritual credits, Jenny. I know we continue to be each other at our Spiritual Root Source. Progress for one is progress for all."

"I kind of like that crazy idea," she told him. It seemed utterly revolutionary in concept to her, completely foreign, exotic. According to her, Jenny only had a state of nonbeing to look forward to when she finally paid for her endless debts—a mountain of debts. Why bother to start? he thought. The job was simply too big. With a system like that, the more you contributed, the guiltier you became—in retrospect—because doing all that service could only mean having a lot of bad karma to repay.

"I think you will attain nirvana," she told him with an encouraging smile.

"What? And altogether cease to be as a unique personality?" he asked.

"If you get lucky, George."

She was deadly serious.

11

The Great Master's Golden Glow

A dozen or so "gainfully employed" Seraphim, somewhere, would have been aware of the fact that Barnard's little firm was to be offered a job that would expose him and his small crew to danger. But there was no advance warning from the Spirit Guardians, although Seraphim supposedly never fail to pass on their messages to the Guardians. Not until George Mathieu had already accepted the job did the nightly eleven-minutes-past-eleven warnings begin.

At the time, as far as George could conclude, the strange 11:11 wake-up calls might be nothing other than some unnecessary cautioning by his own fickle little mortal mind. If handled with care, the slightly radioactive radium represented no real danger to him or his workers. Yet, from the moment the material arrived in his factory, he was awakened each night at eleven minutes past eleven.

Even then, at age twenty-four, he knew there had to be a reason for these mysterious awakenings. It would take him almost ten years to begin to comprehend just what was going on way back then.

In those early days, he suspected his subconscious mind to be scrutinizing future events while he slept. He presumed the wake-up episodes were there to warn him of either opportunities or danger. As another person might awaken in fright from a nightmare, he awoke happily from a simple dream, just to contemplate tomorrow's happenings.

It suited him fine.

Much later, he began to consider the awakenings to be an aspect of the Spirit Guardians' ethical routine to momentarily wake him at that precise time—each time they wanted to infuse data into his mind or, perhaps, had already done so.

The occasional loud voice, clearly discernible and piped into his right ear, might well deal with last-minute advice regarding unforeseen circumstances, he now felt. The 11:11 "programming" during his sleep would deal with circumstances in the making that could easily be foreseen by the brilliantly minded Spirit Guardians.

However, on these six or seven consecutive occasions, and during the period of only one week, he feels, the Guardians were training him to instantly forget what was about to happen.

Years in advance of a brilliant spiritual experience, he was being programmed to put a lesser experience—a prelude to what was to later occur—right out of his mind, almost as soon as it happened.

More than seven years later, the memory of the initial spiritual ecstasy resurfaced. It was then as clear to him as if it had happened on the previous day.

He has named this initial experience the Great Master's Golden Glow.

The young man's name was Marcus—Marc for short—and with his earnest ways, he would go a long way in the business of being a freelance agent. He was open and honest about the dangers associated with the work. But having provided George with all the required information, he still seemed hesitant about leaving Barnard with the job.

"Now, you've got my office number, George," he repeated for the second time. "I'll jot down my home number on the back of my card, just in case. Don't forget, the stuff is radioactive. Don't get it on your skin, or ingest it, or inhale it. And tell your people to be careful with it." It was the fifth time he had warned George of the danger.

"If some of us end up with webbed toes, we won't worry," George told him jokingly. "That won't show. But if we grow an extra set of earlobes, we might get a bit upset, Marc."

The agent gave George another doubtful, troubled look.

"I was only kidding, Marc," he hastened to assure the man. "Make sure we receive all the material in a single delivery, so we can print them all in one large run. I'll supervise the work myself. Quit worrying about it. We'll be careful, truly."

"This job is valued at ten times the amount of my personal worth," Marc admitted. "And I'm new at this job. You can understand, can't you?" he asked.

George told him he understood. The fellow left, feeling confident. At least, he said he was.

Barnard did understand his concern. It had been only a little over three years since he had started his own business. The first year had been tough, and he would never forget what a battle it had been to establish the firm. But the printing they were required to do was now routine for two members of his crew of just eight. Printing a varnish, loaded with radium powder, however, was something new to them all.

Not knowing how much of the radium they would need, Barnard ordered a kilogram of the yellow poison. It was delivered by a courier. Surprisingly, it was packed in a thin, plain paper bag that could easily have ruptured. It was locked away, in a safe place, just as soon as it arrived.

From that night on, until the job was ready to be printed, there was no letup with George's nightly eleven minutes past eleven wake-up calls. He was gradually becoming spooked about the printing job to be performed. He decided not to let anyone else touch the stuff. He worked the entire job by himself, and wore rubber gloves for protection. But perhaps it was only Marc's cautioning that had alarmed him so much. So he thought.

Working till early morning, he completed the printing job. He washed all traces of the radium powder from the machine and put the remaining powder high up on a shelf. Fully seven hundred grams of the superfine, milled radium was left unused. The following morning, he brought a large toughened glass jar with lid and carefully transferred the yellow powder from the paper bag into the jar. The sealed jar went back on top of the shelf, well out of reach. There it stood for ten years or more, shining brightly as the last of the factory lights were switched off at night.

The firm was then growing rapidly, more than doubling its size, year after year. Barnard was usually running two shifts and sometimes even three, right around the clock. But with the central light switches many meters from the main door, the workers and their boss had often bumped into a machine or a mobile work station on their way to lock up for the night. Now the big jar of radium glowed brightly, providing a useful light, for many minutes. It was handy to have it there. There was no more stumbling around in the dark. Bruised and painful shins were a thing of the past for the last person to leave the premises.

∽

More than three years after the completion of that "radium job," George stayed one evening to do some photographic work. Large orders for photographic murals had turned his darkrooms into veritable bottle-necks. Filmwork for printing and photo engraving was falling behind for the first time ever. The firm's mostly female photographers did not work any extra hours because they tended to suffer from the dreaded dark-room syndrome much more quickly than did males. However, they also tended to work their cameras much more efficiently. But now there was simply too much for the women to do. A mountain! Hundreds and hundreds of square meters of photographs.

There was enough camera-ready artwork for George to keep shooting film for hours, with all three different cameras set up for the diverse tasks. He felt happy—strangely full of energy—going about his task, swiftly, routine-like, humming all kinds of tunes. Here was a repertoire of the songs he loved, going back to his childhood days. Such manic, such obsessive, behavior!

Such memory!

He smiled about the thought of his having sudden-ly become obsessive. That would be the jolly day!

I'm just happy! Or am I? Uh? I am elated! But no! That does not explain it either. This is pure rapture!

"Stop and have a coffee," he heard himself say aloud.

"Who needs it?" came the answer, seemingly from another self. The voice was unspoken, and yet heard. There were some fifteen pieces of artwork still to be shot.

"Develop some of the film first," came the sugges-tion. There were now some forty sheets of exposed film ready to be processed.

"Why?" he asked. They were safe in their lightproof boxes. "I'll mix twenty liters of developer and do them all in a row."

He worked on without making test strips. He knew the material too well. "No need for test strips, George Barnard," he heard himself say. He was singing now, remembering the words of long-forgotten songs. They were—to his mind—Georges Brassens's French equiva-lent of gospel songs he had loved, way back then, so long ago. They were there, word for word. The ballads of Edith Piaf, that good-looking "sparrow" with the magnif-icent voice.

Only vaguely did he realize how refreshed and ener-getic he felt. He had been at his job since seven that morning, stayed with the afternoon shift till they left at ten. It was approaching midnight now. And still, he could easily shoot another thirty or forty pieces of artwork and not feel the least bit fatigued. Yet, he could just as easily have reorganized the work and used someone else to shoot the film during lunch breaks—a subcontractor or one of his own crew.

What's the difference? he thought. Why would it matter who does what?

"We are each other," he heard within. It was that same voice that seemed to come from another self. He was amazed.

"What a crazy thing to say!" he reproached the voice, but the truth of it was inescapable.

"We really are each other!" came the immediate response. "Time means nothing. Every aspect of us, every part of us, and every one of us has the very same origin and the very same destiny. We truly *are* each other!"

The voice continued to speak to him, clear and insistent. "Except for a distant yet everywhere-present Creator synthesizing time, space, and the material worlds of our countless universes—by and from the power of Mind alone—we live in a blink-of-the-eye experience that only makes us *look like* individuals. From an Eternity viewpoint, nothing has changed. We are each other!"

George found himself staring back down the long, painful, dismal road of evolution on the planet, and seeing it as a short step. It had happened just a second ago. All of it!

What a ridiculous waste of time to fight wars! he thought. To commit crimes, lie and steal, or be envious of another. How utterly foolish! How nonproductive, negative, shortsighted. My God, what a bloody confused and senseless mess is this rock in space! He was looking up the endless, agonizing, and heartbreaking path towards perfection for all, so far away. And it was so close . . . he could touch it!

He thought of his two children, asleep in their beds. Surely they would be; it was past midnight. "Is there any difference between them and those of the red race, the black race, the yellow race? None! None whatever!" the voice exclaimed.

"They are all mine!" George heard himself say, smiling at the thought of shelling out for their schoolbooks, their music lessons, little braces for unruly little teeth, worldwide. "Good grief!" His life's savings would not cover a day's wear and tear on all their little pairs of shoes. But the realization of humankind's collective responsibility for one another would never diminish from that time on.

It was during that night when his plans for the dispersal of the shares he held in his company took shape. All of his workers would become shareholders in the firm. It seemed to be the least he could do. He was on his way to become the planet's first true communist.

"We are each other at our Spiritual Root Source," Barnard assured the machine on the table in front of him. "And only the illusion of time makes us appear to be individuals. So, now you know. Don't you forget." Anyone wandering into the darkrooms might well be forgiven for thinking George Mathieu was preaching to a most attentive horizontal enlarger as it stood there on its miniature "railway tracks," for he was staring at the thing as he spoke.

Slowly, ever so slowly, he began to realize that the strange state of elation he had felt all night, that feeling of extraordinary energy, must somehow be connected to the ecstasy and feeling of oneness that was now marinating his soul.

Something was about to rapidly bring him back down to earth. Within twenty seconds of his slipping the first few sheets of film into the developer, they all started to turn dark. Only momentarily did the exposed areas of lettering and line-work show up ahead of the background, then the entire sheet turned black. He was shocked, and quickly checked the one-hundred-meter roll from which the sheets were cut. It was the correct roll.

The developer he had only just mixed was the right one to use. The proportions were correct, the temperature spot-on. He checked a dozen safe lights, but there were no telltale emulsion cracks in them, in any of the three darkrooms. He checked the cameras for water condensation, but lenses and condensers were bone dry. It had to be the film. Someone might have made an error, exposing the firm's entire stock of film to white light.

He mixed another small batch of developer and processed a strip of unexposed film, in total darkness, and with a sheet of cardboard covering the little tray. But for a streak of black across the film, emanating from a clearly visible thumbprint—his thumbprint—it remained clear.

It seemed to him that he, himself, was exposing the film. Where else could it have come from?

After some thought, that idea seemed most ridiculous. He switched on all the factory lights and put the photographic rooms in complete darkness. Feeling his way, he spent many long minutes in the dark, but he could not find a single crack in the lightproofing of any of the rooms.

He switched on all the main darkroom lights and put the factory in total darkness. He walked all around the rooms and climbed all over them. Not a glimmer of light was escaping from the photographic department. It was a mystery. It left him dumbfounded. He needed to think, clear his mind. But he needed a cup of coffee more than he needed anything else.

Feeling his way along the walls, he entered the pitch-black lunchroom and froze in shock. Someone was standing there, clearly visible in absolute darkness. This person, this man, was looking at him. As George moved, so did the stranger. With the near-instant realization that he was looking at himself in the lunchroom mirror, he relaxed, but not for long.

He was glowing! Not only was there a glow all around him, his face was emitting light! His hands were emitting light. His clothes were glowing. His jumper, his jet-black woolen jumper, was emitting the same warm, golden light. How can this be possible? he wondered, looking at his glowing image in the mirror in the total darkness of the lunchroom. A most horrible thought struck him. "My God!" he cried. "Oh, Jesus! That bloody radium."

Feverishly, he fumbled his way out of the lunchroom and through the unlit administration block. Visions of a torn brown paper bag with the yellow poison were etching themselves into his mind. Or perhaps some silverfish had finally eaten their way through the paper, and the bag might have spilled its contents. He might have been dusted all over by that horrible stuff. He needed to check the shelves. Stumbling through the production area in panic, tripping over drying racks, cursing his aching shins as he bashed into a machine, he finally turned the corner and looked up.

His mind had played a trick on him, for there stood his still softly glowing glass jar with its nightmare contents safely inside, sealed in by a sturdy stopper, as it had stood there for years. Three years!

That paper bag had once stood in the very same place. Sure enough, it did, but for less than eight hours, until he had safely put the radium in toughened glass. How many times had he looked up at that jar? Hundreds of times. How many of his employees had commented on the usefulness of having it there, and how many times? An untold number.

Now he really needed a coffee. It was urgent. He sat there, sipping the hot brew, puffing away at cigarette after cigarette, staring at himself in the mirror and wondering what had turned him into the biggest glowworm on the planet.

Happy again, laughing now, he said aloud, "What a bright boy you have become, George Mathieu Barnard!"

Finally, he processed all the remaining film-work, just to make sure. It all turned black within the space of some forty to forty-five seconds. He must have been putting out this strange golden light since ten o'clock that evening.

Shortly after two in the morning, the glow faded and then, rather quickly, it was gone. He rounded up all the wasted film and put it in the bin. With it, he presumes, went his memory of what had happened. Recollection of that exciting event would not return for many years. It was simply lifted, truly stolen, from his mind, so he would speak of it to no one.

In the weeks that followed, he put so many black flashes across so many sheets of expensive film that he was quickly barred from his own dark-rooms. His sped-up metabolism wrecked so many expensive watches, he stopped buying and wearing them. But not even the sight of that brightly glowing jar of radium, the only thing visible in his darkened factory, would bring back the memory of the night he glowed. It was erased from his mind.

He remembers now, still. All of it, and in the finest of details—the Great Master's Golden Glow —recognition of his having become a universe-conscious citizen. And with it had come a much-needed boost to his psychic awareness.

How Do We Measure a Human Life?

In Time?
Three-score-years-and-ten?
A century and more?

The length of our lives has no significance.
Each of our lives, from birth to death,
    is less than a blink of the eye of Eternity,
    for Eternity contains all time.
From there we journeyed.
    It continues to be our real home.

To Eternity we return, and with nothing but our
    achievements, our "Universe Credits."

To find that we ever were, still remain, and always will
    be Each Other at our Spiritual Root Source.

part five

✦

The Discovery of the Guardians

The presence of friendly Spirits that Barnard, as a young boy, so often perceived might well have become totally eclipsed in his memory, except for the confrontations he had with his father, which continued until George was about nine. The memories, in fact, persisted quite intact. They became permanently linked to the heated discussions about George giving up those "useless" invisible playmates he was supposed to have outgrown.

True, the tension between Theodore Barnard and his son, George Mathieu, was responsible for the youngster's secrecy—his no longer speaking his mind about his razor-sharp observations of future events. But perhaps this tension wasn't all bad. The boy's sheer stubbornness may well have induced him to prove his father wrong, motivated him to astral travel far and wide, and "invent" so many useful theories of time's anatomy.

In any case, as an adult, he constantly wanted to reacquaint himself with the Guardians he knew had never really gone away. He was now about to revisit them.

You are now being taken back to the time after the Barnards were spared a horrific fate when their insect riddled Gray Eucalypt was safely cut down. George has been "catapulted back to Earth" and survived that hell of an epileptic fit.

As well, Danielle's silver bracelet has been found with the help of "Eureka," but the decision about signing up for the machine parts project has not yet been made.

George will be going back to his university studies as a part-time, mature-age student.

He has made up his mind.

12

"The Name of Our Number. . ."

Many years prior, when George first took up his studies in organizational and normal psychology, one of his favorite lecturers was Edward "Teddy-bear" Willis. Professor Doctor Edward Willis deemed psychology to be an incomplete science.

"Psychologists are only pseudo-scientists," Willis claimed one afternoon, just four or five weeks into the year, as he, Louise Hewitt, and George talked after the lecture. "Those who sailed their longboats a millennium ago knew the Earth to be flat. Did they research their subject? They knew the sun was being transported below the Earth, each night, and with great haste, to shine another day. Had they observed and tracked its path?"

"So, tell me, Miss Hewitt, or you, Barnard, how many of my "do-we-have-to-write-an-essay-about-all-this" and "will-all-that-be-in-the-next-exam" students are researching the whereabouts, the anatomy, and the function of the human spirit, or the soul? And, what other science you two know of avoids the study of the most important components of the subject under observation?"

"Such a hypocrite you are," George told him gruffly. "What fifty-nine-year-old fraud of a psych lecturer bothers to stay on the job for this long?"

It was the kind of pointed question George knew the man appreciated. But with all the gray facial hair Willis sported, and for his looking the other way, Barnard could see nothing of his face. Willis was intentionally ignoring the question for a time, making Barnard sweat. Maybe the student had gone too far in criticizing the man. Louise was holding her breath. She was sure George Mathieu *had* gone too far.

"Tell me, Ted," George insisted. "Where's your real reward?"

"Once in every ten years or so," Willis finally answered, "I meet a George Barnard or a Louise Hewitt, and manage to make them think."

He moved, and in turn looked them in the eyes and said, frowning, "So, what are you?" Then he spun around and simply ambled home without a further word.

Willis could do this sort of thing and let them know they were being paid a compliment, for if you knew this great, spiritually advanced teacher, you knew his heart of gold.

"How lucky can he get?" George asked. "He scored two of us in one year, Lou Lou."

"Oh, God! I died a little when you said that to him. You can be *so* rude!" she complained.

"You already knew he could dish it out. Now you know he can take it, too," George chuckled.

Professor Willis verbally targeted his students about their lack of achievements like a professional soldier fires a deadly weapon at an ill-prepared enemy. He unleashed his devastating judgment on the owner of a data-deficient dissertation like a warplane empties its bomb bay over a sleeping city. Some thought him to be ruthless. Yet, at heart,

Edward Willis was indeed a bit of a teddy-bear, and the best of lecturers.

He was blunt, often providing his students with a rather searching question instead of an appropriate answer.

He forced them all to think.

Parapsychology would always remain his only real interest in life. Few of his students, or even his colleagues, knew. George Barnard somehow found out, and Louise Hewitt had intuitively sensed it a long time before George ever did.

And ruthlessly, the two psychology students took out of his life very many unpaid-for hours of this great master's spare time. From his incredible mind they took all he was prepared to give, readily, uncomplaining, selflessly.

"There is no limit to the capacity of the human spirit and mind," he once told them.

Almost a decade had slipped by since Barnard had seen his lecturer of old. But for Edward Willis's hair having turned a pure white, nothing about him seemed to have changed. He could have long been dead, or retired. Or recycled, George was thinking. If he still has an open mind about reincarnation.

Ted would be sixty-eight years old by now, maybe sixty-nine, George considered. Willis will never die. Someone must take pity on him one day and kindly knock him over the head. Quietly, Barnard was congratulating himself about Willis's still lecturing. Even if half his brain had gone soft by now, he would still be the very best the university had to offer in the field.

Erect behind the big enrollment table, his shoulders straight, Willis was closely scrutinizing the young students one by one and taking their paperwork. Perhaps only one in twenty of the many youngsters in the queue would ever practice as a professional psychologist. That's how it tended to pan out, but all of them would learn so much.

It took fully an hour before it was George's turn to hand over his papers to the man. The professor recognized his former student almost immediately. "What are you working on now, Barnard?" he asked without bothering to say hello.

"A big machine parts contract, a perpetual motion machine, and an appropriate theory for the anatomy of time," George answered without hesitation.

"That chronic attention deficit syndrome of yours is only a mild disorder," Willis suggested bluntly. "You'll live. I wrote down your name. I don't want your papers, because I already know more about you than you will ever know about yourself," he stated gruffly. "And here is your schedule of lectures, which, as you know, will change countless times before we can begin another useless, tortuous round of the same. Oh! But don't go home now. Wait for me outside. I'll be through here in fifteen minutes and I want to talk with you then."

Willis didn't care about Barnard's machine parts contract, or even his perpetual motion machine, but he listened with interest to George's talk about his many theories on the anatomy of time, for many of which the student had invented names.

There was George's Fuzzy Time, Multi-Strand Linear Time, the Coiled Spring, and so many others, the imagined "physiology" of which was so clear in Barnard's mind.

Willis had a more practical approach. "You are spirit, mind and soul," he stated. "Your existence unfolds in that order. You are Eternity and you become Time. When all of what you are is in balance, you will be much better at what you are already doing. At present, life is still happening to you. It is you who are supposed to make life happen. And I am meant to teach you more about these things. You will then be able to return to Eternity with more experiential successes under your belt."

The lecturer had already sensed this was meant to be so, and so had George Mathieu. There was no argument from the businessman.

"You'll be one of only two students," Willis informed him. "I believe you already know the other party."

"I do?"

"The Hewitt girl . . . lady, I should say," Willis corrected himself. "Quite a lady, practicing psychology and about to strike out on her own. Doing a lot better than just the occasional bit of clinical hypnotherapy." There was an evil scowl on his face.

"So very few of us are perfect, Ted," the occasional therapist suggested. George, delighted with the news, was looking forward to seeing Louise again.

"Thick as thieves you two were," Willis grunted. "I thought. . ."

"Wrong! Whatever it was you were thinking. We are siblings of a kind, is all."

Night after night of spare-time private tuition followed. Together with his co-student of years ago, the Hewitt lady—now married and the mother of a tiny new person—he learned to drop the metabolism of his brain and mind to incredible depths. They communicated mind to mind, and dowsed for gold and oil fields on maps. The two succeeded in slowing down or racing their hearts at will, even letting them skip a few beats on command.

They attended sweat lodges, walked over white-hot, one-thousand-degree fires, and learned to bend one-inch-thick steel rods with the use of their minds alone. It was all designed to teach them to exercise complete control over their minds.

They both thought it would all quickly come to an end and hence they would be teaching themselves whatever else they needed to know.

They were so wrong.

"You will meet your Spirit Guide or Guides this evening," Willis stated. "Call them what you like . . . Guardians . . . whatever. . . See them as real or imaginary, it matters not a bit. Your eyes closed, in a deep trance, you will come face to face with those who will now guide you throughout your lives. They are totally impartial, and you can bounce your ideas and theories off them. Then take to heart the answers that come your way. Have faith in the veracity of what they tell you, always.

"Let's go. Let yourselves drift now. Let yourself drift deeper and deeper. Now enter that misty, pleasant scene of nature in your mind. And let the mist clear now. . . slowly now."

The figure was standing on a rocky outcrop—a tall, powerfully built, near-naked Spirit Sentinel holding a spear with a large, shimmering, spearhead.

He could be a Native North American or just as easily have Negro blood, Barnard mused. It was hard to tell. The light was poor and there was just a faint trace of color in all George saw. But the details of what the mortal perceived on the screen of his mind were sharp. The Warrior was scanning the distant horizon and was either unaware of his being watched, or choosing to ignore the human.

A gray hide tied around his waist, reaching to just above the knees, was all the Sentinel wore. This Combatant in bare feet, Barnard guessed, would be thirty, say thirty-two at most. Near enough my age, he mused. He eyed the awesome weapon with some concern, but felt he could trust the Warrior.

This well-armed Fellow did not at all look like the Spirit Friends George remembered from his youth. He saw this Spirit Guardian as nothing more than the soul of someone long departed. Such a great shame he died in his prime, Barnard thought. He appears to have been somebody of great potential—a mighty hunter of men and beasts.

The Guardian was picking up on the mortal's thoughts, Barnard knew. And as the Spirit Guide with his dangerous-looking spear slowly turned to face him, George could tell that the Warrior was not at all amused about being judged to have expired at some time in the past. This Guardian knew a great deal about the human. George sensed he did. But the human knew nothing about the Guardian.

"I greet you, friend, and my name is George Mathieu Barnard," the mortal framed his thoughts.

"We greet you," came the instantaneous mind-to-mind reply, "and we all ways know you."

That was a tricky answer! Does he know everything about me or has he always known me? George wondered. Or is it both of these? Although they were communicating mind to mind, there was no doubting the Guardian's command of the English language, despite his choosing to only use present tense.

"So, what's your name then?" George casually asked of the Guardian's mind. Surely, he thought, you might have volunteered that information by now.

It surprised the human when the Guardian spoke. "Ahbécétutu," he said out loud and quickly.

George was almost sure Ted Willis and Louise had heard it, too. Despite his being in a deep trance, his mind was racing. Any name with *tut* in it might well be Egyptian, but he doesn't look like a being of that ancient race. Barnard was puzzled. Speaks about himself in the plural? he mused. Thinks of himself as royalty?

"What's your surname then?" George asked. Getting the answer to that will quickly clear things up, he considered, and will place him somewhere on some continent.

"Ahbécétutu!" the Guardian answered, much louder than before. He was seemingly troubled by George's lack of understanding, or the little trust the air-breathing mammal was affording him.

Poor fellow, Barnard thought. He must have had

just the one name. And a strange one at that—it ends with the name of a ballerina's skirt. But where does it come from? A thought struck him. He might be both Bantu and Zulu, and somehow these two names had gotten themselves mixed up.

But the mere thought of this was enough for him to learn from the Sentinel's eyes that George Mathieu had got it all wrong again. This Spirit Warrior was not going to volunteer any more information on the subject.

Barnard gave it one more try. "Can you spell it for me?" his mind requested.

"It is never written!" came the abrupt response. Ahbécétutu, or whoever he was, was growing tired of those questions about his name.

Never written? Not yet written? the mortal wondered. Never to be written? Or "don't you dare write it down or I'll stick this spear through you?" Could he have predated all forms of written language? Barnard gave up. "Shall I just call you Bzutu, for short?" he asked. "Is that fine with you? Giving every foreigner with a difficult-to-pronounce name a nickname is somewhat of a tradition in Australia. I got used to it. Man! You would not believe how badly my name gets mutilated in this country."

The Guardian's big smile and glistening white teeth told him there was no problem with the nickname. Barnard had got lucky. This was a friendly Spirit Guardian. Even if he was long dead, he seemed to have retained his sense of humor.

"From where did you hail, Bzutu?" George asked, feeling more confident.

Instantly a map appeared on the screen of the human's mind, and a point broadly east-northeast of the Mediterranean lit up in a flash. The next moment, it was gone. Nothing of what he was telling his human charge was making an iota of sense, but the colorful mind-to-mind pictures he was transmitting were a wonder to behold. The Warrior was brilliant at doing that. *If* he was doing it.

"So, what did you do for a living?" Barnard's mind asked.

Again, Bzutu spoke: *"I am Warrior. I am Chief. I am Shaman. I am Teacher."* He seemed to reiterate he was still very much alive, hardly a part of history.

Why don't you pull the other leg? thought the businessman. George Barnard was beginning to doubt whether what he was viewing and hearing had anything to do with reality. If you said you were thirty-five years of age, Mister, he thought, I might still believe you. But all those professions? That's an all-time, almighty rise through the ranks.

This Spirit Guardian seemed to know his every thought. He seemed to also sense the mortal's frustration. "I am One Thousand, One Hundred and Eleven," he said at last, *"the name of our Number, the number of our Name. We share your space, not your time. I am Ahbécétutu."*

Finally! Finally, something made sense. Suddenly, something was making a whole lot of sense! An overwhelming amount of sense.

This Warrior really was the mortal's Teacher, and responsible for teaching his mammalian student things of the future, perhaps even the wacky theories of time. All those years of eleven-minutes-past-eleven phenomena had been his doing. They were his courtesy wake-up calls, telling his flesh-and-blood pet vertebrate that something was about to be infused into his subconscious mind, to later surface at the appropriate time. Or perhaps it was to let him know the transferral of data had already been completed.

Barnard still rather doubted that one who had died so young had had so many professions. But, accepting that he had really been a warrior, a chief, and a shaman, as well as a teacher, had his behavior always been morally appropriate? The human wanted to know.

His newfound Friend seemed not very impressed with—but hardly distressed about—his own achievements during "the time when there is no Law." His present behavior was closely scrutinized by his Seraphic Superiors and deemed to be flawless.

"I am all ways vouched for," came yet another mind-to-mind answer.

"In all ways," George Barnard mumbled. Eh! Friend! I actually got that message!

His interview with the near-naked Guide had come to an end, it seemed. Barnard's attention was directed to a new personality who had appeared on the scene of his mind. Seated in an ancient, solid wooden chair, this individual appeared to be neither male nor female but both. Although appearing in a more distant, foglike time frame than Bzutu's, he, she—or it—was endowed with well-developed breasts, as well as a sparse beard. Barnard was rather startled by what his eyes were now slowly making out. Undoubtedly, it raised the level of his metabolism, and the experience almost ended right then. With his eye contact with Bzutu interrupted, communication was decidedly hampered.

It would take him days to wake up to the fact that he was being told that here was a truly androgynous individual. But at the time, Barnard misunderstood. He thought he was being informed that the name of this personality was Andréa.

Numbers and codes were being flashed to his mind, but he rejected the concept of numbers instead of names, even for Spirit Guardians. People have names and, at the time, he saw them as people who had at some time in their past lost their physical bodies.

George's attitude towards the strange "bisexual" creature was poor, deplorable, even shameful. He would later apologize to the Guardian and soon learn to admire the phenomenal brilliance of Andréa's mind.

George's eyes swung back to the one he had nick-named Bzutu who, by reflecting his thoughts onto the mortal's mind, was able to show him what he, the Spirit Guide, was seeing. There, standing right behind George's chair, it was clearly intimated, stood someone he should already know—a brilliant Being of light—with a form outlined in space by myriad multicolored points of light, all scintillating with life.

Here was the Being responsible for the records of his life, he was told. Here was someone with a code of numbers as long as his arm. With lots of ones, fours, and sevens, and George could actually make them out. Here was a Seraph, a Guardian Angel, a Creature without wings.

Invisible to human eyes, her image was transferred to his trance-enhanced awareness by the thought reflection of Ahbécétutu's powerful mind. The Spirit Guide perceived the Seraph with great ease, although she was obviously even more distant in time than was Andréa. It was made clear to the human that she enjoyed the French language, which George had long neglected.

Presumptuously, he instantly named her Juliette—a typically French name, with straight-sided letters replacing her straight-sided numbers—her ones, fours, and sevens.

A fourth personality was hardest of all to discern. The shimmering blue form was decidedly female, but Barnard decided she might well be a figment of his imagination, and thus did not request to know her name. It would take years from that night for him to finally conclude that this was Simone. This was Danielle's "imaginary playmate," but in fact also a member of the group, and a lightning-fast Messenger with a great sense of humor.

There was one last mind-to-mind communication from the Warrior: *"Remember the future."*

"What does that mean?" George wanted to know of him. "How can anyone remember the future?" But Ahbécétutu was quickly lost from view as Professor Willis guided his two students out of the near-death trance.

"I always *thought* my Spirit Guide was called John!" Louise exclaimed when she popped up from her trance, her cheeks all rosy. "Now I know what he looks like, too. I'm so excited!" She was ever so pleased with having discovered a new Friend. She glanced at Barnard. "How did you go, George?" she asked.

"I met enough guys to start my own soccer team," he answered. "All of them much better players than I. They all had numbers on their jerseys, but I didn't catch their names, Louise. Say, do you think guardian angels have wings?"

Edward Willis looked like he had caught on, but he never said a word.

It was to be the last of the two students' private meditation lessons with him.

Soon after, George's work as a clinical hypno-therapist was to bring him into contact with yet another Spirit Guardian. True to form, the dreamer of a mortal once again rejected the use of any kind of code, and it was then suggested that he'd better call the Guide by the very human name that he had apparently taken on.

Even as a child, Barnard had given every single one of his numerous pets a name. Nothing much had changed in his attitude towards any personality in his life as an adult. Spirit Guardians, he felt, were surely entitled to have names if rabbits did.

Much later, George Mathieu finally broke the obvi-ous alphabetical/numerical code.

In the days following, Barnard would learn that Bzutu never ages, never sleeps, and never for-gets. George would clearly grasp linear time to be a product of Eternity, without understanding the "manufacturing process" or how his Spirit Friends could hide within alternative facets of time. But he now knew how to bridge the gap and make visu-al contact.

He also gave much thought to Bzutu's advice to "remember the future." There could be many meanings, such as: "Remember your reasons for being . . . for living" or "Take note of our advance warnings and advice." But if remembering the future would prove to be too difficult in the end, he could always do the next best thing and simply forget the past.

The advice, if meant in this way, would have been most appropriate for him at that time in his life. George had long ago suffered a major health setback. He had been the victim of a vicious attack by a crazed drug addict. Beaten unconscious, he had been left to die, but he had tenaciously clung to life. He was well on his way to a near complete recovery, though often still in pain.

The only remaining serious problem he needed to deal with was those sporadic epileptic fits. These fits could occasionally be violent and life-threatening. He was also still angry, unforgiving, about what he had been made to suffer.

Bzutu's wisecrack about remembering the future might well have been a suggestion to put the past to rest. But perhaps a great number of other meanings also had merit.

Even though the mortal would almost daily communicate with the Spirit Guardians from this time onwards, there would never be an explanation for remembering the future.

The brilliantly minded Guardian was indeed his Teacher. Like Professor Willis, Bzutu forced the vertebrate to think.

I Would Like to Know

If you are setting a place at the dinner table
    for your very own, personal Spirit Guide,
    and you are watching the tasty morsels disappear
    into fresh air as he consumes your delicious food,
I would like to know about it.

If your personal Guardian of the Halfway Realm
    takes over the chauffeuring
    when peak-hour traffic gets on your nerves,
    tell me about it. I'd love to know.

And if you are regularly taking a shower
    with the Seraph who has been appointed
    to the task of monitoring the progress
    of your time/space existence,
    and you take turns scrubbing each other's backs,
    I'd like to hear from you as well.

I said I wanted to know about it.

I didn't say I would believe you.

6

The Celestial-Mortal Alliance

In the quiet and semi-darkened clinic, George Mathieu pushed his body back in the patients' reclining chair. As he imagined the gentle urgings of Willis's voice, the metabolism of his brain and mind plunged to more closely synchronize with the time frame of the Spirit Guardians.

The mortal conjured up a cozy little office with a chair and a desk, complete with an antique telephone. In his mind he reached out to it, dialed 1111, and sensed the signal whizzing around the globe. There were many questions to be asked and many answers to be obtained from those who were now known to be his Teachers.

The Spirit Guardians were taking their time.

"This is as deep as I can safely go," Barnard grunted. "Any more relaxed and I'd be dead. Any deeper and my heart will stop pumping, I'll stop breathing, and the last spark of life will leave my neglected body. Where are you Guys?"

Suddenly, the Warrior materialized on the screen of his mind. No more than a few paces from his flesh-and-blood student he stood, a serious look on his face. Ahbécétutu was quite alone, it seemed.

"You haven't aged a bit since I saw you yesterday,

Bzutu," the mortal tried. "There's a chair for you, just to your right. Take the weight off your feet. You've been on the go for a long time since your last catnap, I bet."

The mortal's humor was lost on the Guardian. The Spirit Guide shifted his weight and leaned more heavily on his spear. It was clear he would not respond and play the mortal's childish game.

"You're not in the mood, I can see. I'll come to the point," Barnard informed him. "I have many questions, my Friend. Why have you selected me to work with you?"

"You select us," came the mind-to-mind answer.

"But I didn't know any of you," Barnard countered. "You mean I volunteered?"

"It is so," the Warrior replied.

The mortal was puzzled by the Guardian's response. "I'm not complaining, but I don't recall."

"Think. Remember," he was told. There was obviously no more to be said on the subject. The Spirit Guardian seemed pressed for time. He wanted away.

"I will try to remember," Barnard replied. "But tell me. . . this big machine parts contract—what would you decide?"

"You decide," came the swiftly expressed mind-to-mind retort.

"I'm only human," the mortal countered. "We're an enterprising lot, but we're also full of fears. We don't live on fresh air, you know. We need food, clothing, housing, and lots of other things. It all costs money. And we could go broke on that project."

"You decide!" came the impatient reply.

"Okay, okay, okay. Just tell me what it is we're

working on next," he wanted to know. "What's on your unwritten list, Bzutu?"

"We guide you," came the abrupt answer. Then the Guardian was gone.

You just do as you're told, mortal, thought Barnard. We cooperate, but it's all a one-way deal. He swiftly realized it was far from the truth.

Quickly surfacing from the trance, he went on in the Guardian's role: "You're only human, George. Just another mammal. One step up from a chimp. So, what do you expect? Written instructions?"

"Well, I was actually going to offer you a share in the new business, Bzutu," he grunted his reply at his already departed Companion. "But seeing you don't have any pockets to stash the profits in, what's the bloody use?"

How can I volunteer for something I've never even heard of? he asked of his own mind. "Think! Remember!" Bzutu had urged him.

Easily said.

Later that evening, he did remember having put himself in the firing line. It really was George Mathieu who had stuck his neck out. No one had conscripted him into a platoon of Spirit Guardians.

He had indeed volunteered.

13

Maria Morgan

A strong swimmer used to the cold Atlantic waters, George Mathieu dived into the surf without hesitation. Australia's Palm Beach in September was deserted as far as the eye could see. The water of the South Pacific was simply too cold for the locals at that time of the year, and the board-riders preferred to be elsewhere on that day. Within minutes, he knew he was in danger of drowning, but was unwilling to admit it to himself.

A powerful rip was speeding him out to sea. There would be no one to rescue the lone swimmer. Someone would discover his vehicle and clothing, perhaps even his body, tomorrow, eventually, but much too late.

He could see the beach receding from view. He struggled for all he was worth, but minutes later as he glanced up, the safety of white sands was easily a kilometer away. He was being sucked into the Pacific Ocean at a rate of knots.

"I'll flaming well be in New Zealand for supper," he heard himself say. "I should have brought my passport. Such disregard for travel regulations!"

Instantly, he realized he was poking fun at himself and the desperate plight he was in. "What a damned fool you are, George Mathieu Barnard!"

He battled on.

A successful businessman, just twenty-two years of age, drowned at picturesque Palm Beach today, came an imaginary radio broadcast. *Police were left the unenviable task of informing the young man's grief-stricken fiancée of this, yet another, tragedy on our many unpatrolled beaches.*

There was now a layer of sea mist obscuring the coast, and George Mathieu had progressed at least another four hundred meters towards the Shaky Isles. It was time for him to face reality—or panic, big-time.

"Christ! You've gotta get me . . . out of this!" he shouted, out of breath, choking now, his mouth suddenly full of brine. He spat it out. "Get me out of this!"

He turned and swam towards a rocky land-tongue with a sudden, newfound strength that was never his own. Calmness came over him, born from the instant knowledge that he would be safe.

Finally, exhausted, he clung to a sharp oyster-covered rock for many minutes before he risked hoisting himself to bruising and bloodletting safety. Relieved and feeling ever so small, he sat there catching his breath and inspecting the deep gashes the oyster shells had inflicted on him. But he had been triumphant. He had fought and won a two-hour battle with the ferocious current for the prize that was his life. He also knew he had not been alone. Not for a single second.

"Forget what I promised You about going back to church," he told the Big Man in charge of the local universe. "That was a stupid spur-of-the-moment bribe to get You to get me out of the soup. You know I hate churches, endless boring sermons, icy-cold and rock-hard pews. Let me dedicate my life to the welfare of other people. I can handle that."

He knew Someone, somewhere, would second the motion.

But life went on at an ever more hectic pace, and Barnard soon forgot his sacred pledge. Others remembered.

From this long-ago pact, one might presume, eventuated the association with the Spirit Guardians of the unseen realms of time. Within weeks, the eleven-minutes-past-eleven courtesy wake-up calls commenced.

The therapist had become the unworthy recipient of the Great Master's Golden Flame, with all its ecstasy and privileges, all its agony and responsibilities. He had become the healer dear old Ethel, Swami Sarasvati, and Janelle Gillies long ago knew he would be.

People would soon be coming to him by the hundreds to be healed. Sure! Sure! He could see it in his mind's eye. He would casually walk past them, touch them on the forehead in turn, and say, "You're healed. You're done as well. Remember to water your cacti. You're fine. And you, too, can go home. Oh, be kind to your pet poodle."

But the hype had worn off, and still nothing was happening. The promise of the Golden Flame appeared to have been a fake—the most evil double-cross perpetrated in the annals of the local universe. So he thought—then he forgot about it.

Why had George Barnard gone to that official university dinner? Why would he waste all evening on a live play reported to be quite boring? He was only a part-time student who belonged to none of the boarding colleges and was just associated with one. He had never before agreed to join Louise Hewitt at her old college's tables on evenings like this. Why would he consent? God only knows . . . but Barnard was there with her.

Their meals had just been brought to the table.

George noticed someone just a few tables away, who looked quite gray. There appeared to be two of her, side by side. She's literally beside herself, he thought, but with what? The searing pain of a migraine shot through his head. His stomach was in uproar. His food suddenly tasted bland. That isn't me! he realized with a start. It is she! I am taking on that woman's symptoms. Things like that had happened all too often, but never to that degree.

"It's brilliant cooking, George," Louise remarked, "hoe into it. You're only picking at your food." She looked him in the eyes. "You look ill, pale. Do you have an ulcer or something?"

He carefully shook his aching head. "They're someone else's symptoms," he mumbled. "She's over there, two tables across, facing us and a little off to the right. See her? Next to the guy with the wavy brown hair. The woman in gray."

"She's wearing blue, George," Louise informed him. "She's wearing a bright blue pant-suit. I talked with her earlier."

That came as a surprise. Barnard had another good look at her, but she looked gray to him. The whole dining hall looked like an out-of-focus color photograph with a small gray picture inserted where she sat. She, too, was only picking at her food. Maybe I should get the new lenses in my glasses checked out, he thought. But he knew that wasn't it. He needed to go and touch her on the forehead. That would make her migraine go away. Here, at last, was the promise of the Great Master's Golden Flame to be fulfilled.

"Her name is Maria Morgan," Louise informed him. "I played a few games of tennis with her this year. She's doing year two, Human Resources, I think. She's a part-time student, like we are. And I think the fellow next to her is her husband. He once came to pick her up." She added, "They've got two children, but they've been at each other's throats for years. That's what Maria told me."

"Who else do you know at that table?" George asked.

Louise looked again at the diners, but she didn't recognize anyone else, only Maria Morgan. What a coincidence that is, he thought.

"I'll have to fix her migraine, Lou Lou," he said. "Then we can both enjoy our dinner." He tried to get up, but he couldn't. He was stuck fast in his chair, it seemed. How annoying. "Do me a favor, please, Louise," he asked her. "Go tell the Morgan lady that when she has had enough of that cross-eyed headache, I'll take it away from her. It's pounding my brains to bits as well."

Louise left to talk to Maria and soon returned. "Maria says thanks, George, and if it gets any worse, she'll come and see you."

George's migraine had lessened somewhat, but he knew she still had to be healed that evening.

George and Louise finished their dinners and filed into the theater. The Morgans' reserved seats were precisely next to theirs—in a five-hundred-seat theater—how strangely coincidental. But soon after Maria seated herself, she collapsed onto the floor. Her wavy-haired husband never bothered with her. What a sweetheart! The man simply stood aside, as though he were a total stranger, to let someone else take care of his wife.

With the help of one of the bouncers, Barnard carried the rather heavy woman to the ladies' rest room. One of the female ushers moved ahead of them and opened all the doors. They placed the almost entirely unconscious Maria on a couch. Barnard told the bouncer he would have her back in the land of the living in no time, and he asked the young lady to stay.

There must have been something for her to learn from him, but George himself didn't know what it was. And what followed next must have left the usher with more questions than answers.

With his fingers on Maria's temples, his thumbs on her forehead, as he had long ago been programmed to do, he told her what she needed to know. She learned about what her future held and what she needed to do. Search the healer for the words he used. He had no idea about what he was telling her.

Maria Morgan was receiving a stream of information that never slowed for many minutes. The young lass stood behind him as if nailed to the ground, listening to all he had to say. Barnard was only listening to the echo of his voice, wondering who was making him say all those things. But he knew the information was correct.

Finally, the job was done. Maria Morgan sat up on the couch, saying, "Gee, I feel good! I'll go and do all that!" There was a glow about her, and George now realized she was indeed wearing blue. It really suits her, he thought. But he wondered what it was he had said and done.

Maria said, "That was very clever of you, George." And then she hopped from the couch and went back to watch the show.

"What do you call that—what you just did?" the usher asked Barnard.

"I have no name for it," he told her. "It's something that just happens. A healing."

"Who's doing that healing then?" she insisted on knowing. "I wanted to see it better, but I couldn't move. How did that happen?"

George pointed at the ceiling and told her, "They're doing it up there. It actually has nothing to do with me. I do what I'm told to do and say what I'm told to say. Spirit Guardians and Seraphim do all the work."

Shortly after, back in the theater, Maria Morgan stood and told her husband, "We're going home." He didn't like that idea and complained. She told him bluntly, "You've got some surprises coming." They left.

⤳

During the days that followed, George Mathieu remembered more and more of what he had told Maria Morgan that evening. She was to take her children and leave her husband. Louise later confirmed she had done just that. It perturbed the therapist, endlessly, to have been involved in the ending of that marriage. But there was no more marriage anyway. Maria's husband had found another woman and he was fully committed to her. Still, even then it troubled George.

Not until much later, when he finally bothered to check with the Spirit Guardians, did he
learn why Maria had to leave. There was a large,
tortured artery or vein in her brain. The way she
was being mistreated by her husband—ever more
violently as their disagreements became more
physical—she was becoming a prime candidate
for a massive stroke. As he was shown this, he
realized he had already seen that blood vessel, and
had been told that she would not survive for much
longer. This had simply faded from his mind until
now.

Now that he knew exactly how to do these
healings—a standard procedure—he expected
many more, all of them like Maria Morgan's. He
somehow knew he could count on it.

But in all the years that followed, the healing
of Maria Morgan was to be the only one of its
kind. All those that followed were vastly different,
for this universe never let up in providing the rookie of the Spirit Guardian's platoon with surprise
after surprise.

The Gods deserve a good laugh from time to
time. Why not at a mortal's expense? And why
begrudge them their fun?

14

"You Must Believe Me!"

"I suppose you're pleased that our stint with Professor Willis is over?" Jodi Barnard suggested at their Thursday evening dinner. It had been a statement as much as a question. She knew her husband was exhausted. "Did you and Louise learn anything?"

"We learned stacks, Jodi." Barnard assured her. "We both got visual proof of there being life in the Halfway Realm, but the natives provide only monosyllabic answers if they can get away with it. They also keep a tight lid on planned future projects, and on top of that, they totally lack business acumen." He gave her a sly grin. "I offered one of them a directorship in the company. And guess what?"

"What?"

"He knocked it back without a moment's hesitation. That kind of attitude doesn't do much for our human-celestial relationship, does it?"

She offered him one of those tired, raised-eyebrow glances.

"Knowing these Guardians by their looks hasn't really changed anything much. Say, since you knew what 'Eureka' meant," Barnard carried on, "would you happen to know what an Emen-ohwait is? I've heard that word three times in the last few weeks, when treating patients who have been in St. Clare's Hospital. A bit strange, that."

He paused, needing to give the matter some thought. Jodi was ignoring him, expecting another of his dumb tricks, and understandably so. Her husband missed few opportunities to cause a stir.

"In the clinic, Jodi," Barnard went on. "I'm sure I heard it right. I'm not fooling! Did you by any chance take any calls from St. Clare's in the last month or so?"

She only shook her head in answer, still distrustful of him.

"Because some doctor there is referring patients to come and see me," he told her. "And whenever I'm with one of them, I hear that word. All of them are tough cases. Attempted suicides. But I don't even know that doctor. So far, I don't even have his name."

Again, Jodi shook her head, still looking doubtful.

"My father says," the little one advised her mother, "if you don't know the answer, you have to pull a face like a stunned mullet. Like this." She was pulling a cleverly distorted face at her mother.

"Oooh! How very ugly is a mullet fish!" Jodi told her.

Right then, the doorbell rang, and instantly all three children ran to answer the door, leaving their parents alone at the table.

Jodi was furious about their lack of manners. Slowly, deliberately, she put down her knife and fork. She placed her elbows on the table, cupped her face in her hands, and said ever so softly, "Now you see them . . . now you don't."

"Just like the Spirit Guardians," George agreed. "Elusive, mysterious, evasive."

The little one was the first to return. "It's an old woman and she's crying."

"No, it's a skinny lady with long, red hair," the boy disagreed.

Moments later, Danielle returned. "It's a young lady, and she looks very sad. She wants you, Dad. I pointed to the clinic and switched on the lights for her."

Barnard sighed and shrugged. At least he had had enough time to empty his plate. "Thanks a lot, all of you children—I think. Two patient-free nights in a row is an unacceptable waste of human resources," he suggested. "But there's still tomorrow night. Leave my sweets in the refrigerator, please, Jodi."

Her large, deep-green eyes looked dull and pained, and as he entered the clinic, her brief smile was synthetic. She had found a place on a couch in a corner of the big room, away from his desk. Holding a small black purse, she was clasping her navy-blue skirt tightly around her knees.

She looked skittish, prepared to run off at a moment's notice. Coiled up like a spring on the very edge of that settee, she resembled a hunted, cornered quarry—a feral animal about to be culled.

"I'm George Barnard," he told her, "but you knew that already. I drink gallons of black coffee to awaken my brain, and you didn't know that. Yours is white, one sugar, I'm sure." He took two cups from the shelf and set about making the brew, wondering if she would speak to him, or contradict him. She didn't.

"It might be ever so useful if I knew your name, Miss, uh. . ." he suggested.

"Mrs. My name is Leonie. White and just a little sugar, that's how I like it." It was the voice of a child and the voice of an old woman, both.

What untold misery did this planet bring you? he wondered. You could be twenty-five or forty-five. Who could tell? Your hair cut, thinned out, and layered would improve your looks. With it done up high in pins and combs and clips and stuff, you would look so very pretty. A little rouge, lipstick, mascara, and eye shadow, and you'd steal someone's heart. Who are you hiding from, making yourself look so dull?

He handed her the coffee. "As ordered, Missy. This will stimulate your mind and presently lubricate your vocal cords as well." He waited for her, decided he was standing too close to her, and moved back. She needed a huge comfort zone.

"All I want is to talk to you," she said. "Just talk, nothing more. No one ever listens to me. They look like they do, but they don't. They never do." She sipped at her drink, and he gave her the space. "Sometimes they listen, sure enough," she contradicted herself, "but then they don't believe me. 'Have a tranquilizer, old girl, you'll feel much better tomorrow.'"

She started to sniff a little. Her small purse yielded an amazing supply of pure white tissues. She had come prepared. She put them on her lap, then clamped her hands around the hem of her skirt again. "Yeah, yeah, pop another pill. They'll make you feel good and sick in the end. But no one ever listens to me. . ."

"Wrong century, Leonie," he informed her. "You have arrived in a time and a place when and where the people are all deaf. This is the age of communication and we all know how to talk, but we forget to listen. For goodness sake! Did you not know this?"

"I want *you* to listen to me," she insisted. "One person! Just you . . . and don't stop me to ask questions." She softly sniffed into a paper towel. "I hate questions!" she shouted. "They show that people don't understand and they don't want to understand."

"Fine!" he told her sharply. "I listen and that's all I do. You talk and start making sense. If you don't, watch it, woman. I'll let you have it."

Her reaction to his harsh words surprised him. Mrs. Leonie Whoever was taking him up on the challenge. There was light in those sad eyes, a hopeful expression on her face, and she visibly relaxed in an instant.

What's going on? He had directed this question to the minds of the Spirit Guardians. How can she be as straight as a die, when I feel I'm being waylaid here? Help me, you Guys.

"Listen to her!" came the reply from within his mind.

"Just listen to me," echoed her voice. "No one listens. No one has the time."

She sniffed some more and dried her eyes, then focused on a point in space. Seemingly she needed to do that to be able to concentrate. She took a deep breath and appeared to have plucked up the needed courage.

"My mother was a heavy drinker. Whisky, thank you very much. Drunk as a skunk she was, most of the time, and a bit off as well, and worse as time went on. My father couldn't hack it any more. He left us and went interstate. But he left me too! And I did nothing wrong!"

She looked at George for support, but he was voluntarily tongue-tied. He nodded to confirm he was listening.

"I was only six! Only six, George!"

Keeping his mouth shut wasn't working. "You ate your sticky porridge every day," he suggested. "That's all I ever ask of any six-year-old. At six, you're a kid."

Somewhat heartened by his casual attitude, she moved ever so remotely towards him, then thought better of it and slid back. She shot him a nervous little smile and carried on as her eyes found that point in space again.

"My mother got to drinking more all the time and acting queer, till they locked her away. Never there when I came home from school, and sometimes she left me some food, sometimes some money. Mostly nothing, and then she brought her boyfriends home, and I had to stay in my room or else I'd get locked in. When the guy finally left, she'd wake me up and we'd go out and get something to eat and more whisky for her to pack away at night. Too spaced-out to cook or do the washing. All that, and make the beds—hers too—and clean the house. I had to do it all. But when she fleeced her boyfriends, I got a really good meal—midnight, mostly."

Her sad eyes swung back to him. She was begging him for a little understanding, but hardly for herself.

"She was a prostitute," he told her bluntly. He shrugged. "It does so happen, Leonie."

"She was my *mother* . . . and she *loved* me! George?" Wide-eyed, she stared at him, shocked by what he had said, pleading for a kind word for the memory of a loved one, frightened stiff of the truth.

"Fine," he told her. "That's how I see it. She was your mother. She did love you very much. She was a whore and a piss-pot, as well. Those are facts, Leonie. That is reality! But I will not judge her for what she did, and neither must you. Only face up to the sad truth of it all. So, why don't you face it and say it, perhaps."

She seemed undecided, apprehensive, then she spoke, softly, "She was a prostitute and an alcoholic"— sounded as if she were swallowing the words—"but she *was* my mother and she loved me very, *very* much!" She was biting her lips and needed to reflect on the statement she had made. "I've never said anything like that. Why do I feel good about saying that?" She frowned and looked confused by her own feelings. "I wouldn't dare think that, let alone. . . *It is the truth!*"

"Good!"

She was waiting for his further comments.

"It's your session," he reminded her. "And I hate questions as much as you do."

"Yes," she answered, as if vaguely recalling the deal that was struck, "of course. My mom got into trouble with the police, just trouble. Later on, she got arrested a few times for putting bricks through shop windows and things like that. She got worse, and in the end they put her in an asylum, after she went on another binge, after drying out. The Child Welfare people came to get me, and I was so frightened. I was nine then, and I had heard all the stories. But it was all right, really. Lots of kids around, regular meals and—hard to believe—but I got to be as round as a barrel. Look at me now. . ."

She paused for a while, needing to reflect, or find some courage. Suddenly her mind seemed made up. "They're related to me. My maternal grandfather and my husband's father are—well, Grandpa died—were half-brothers, and they are the people who adopted me. They came to get me, and at first it was good to have a home and a family and to belong somewhere. And then he started to interfere with me. And his wife knew and just let him do it. She never said anything! She never wanted to know about it, ever. I was less than ten years old when he raped me, and I thought I would die. I'm thirty-three now, George, and nothing has changed."

She raised her voice in anger at her desperation, "I get raped and raped and raped and raped!" Her angry shouts then almost dropped to a whisper, "And I die each time. They own me . . . I die each time. . ." Her eyes full of tears, she stared at him in fear of being disbelieved, ridiculed, despised, or of being ordered to leave the clinic.

His mind was racing, searching. My God, what have I got here? Is this the truth? Am I hearing this? This is either the most brilliant deception or the worst thing ever.

"Get the hell out of the place!" he snapped at her.

"I . . . can't!" she shouted back through her tears. "I've got a husband. I've got a father-in-law. They both use me!" Tears were running down her cheeks. Her face contorted, her nose running, she didn't bother to dry her tears. She kept blinking them away and looking at him in fear.

Strangely out of breath, she shouted, "I've got . . . four children too!" Then her voice became a sobbing whisper, "And I don't . . . even know . . . who their fathers are. . ."

Slowly her head bent forward to almost touch her knees, and so she stayed, helpless, hopeless, and broken. Her body rocked as she sobbed and sniffed over a life-time of human misery—a ruthless sentence without end.

"Shit!" he swore. He quickly moved to hold her hand as she blindly reached out to him.

"I . . . hurt," she cried, but she kept hiding her face in her lapful of tissues. "I'll go now . . . if you don't . . .

believe me," her painful gasps told him.

"No, Leonie, you stay. You talk and I listen, as I promised I would. And I'm right here holding your hand."

She let go of his hand almost immediately. Again, she needed her space, and Barnard backed off again.

"Give me a second. . . I'll be okay," she sniffed.

"I'm going to top up our coffees, young lady."

"Good! You have to hear it all." She quickly glanced at him, then turned her swollen eyes away to dry her tears, suddenly ashamed of having lost control over her emotions. ". . . hear it all . . ." she mumbled.

He walked away from her to make more coffee and to give himself a badly needed break. He needed to think, evaluate, find a solution. What is this? Is it incest? Forced prostitution? A whole liturgy of crime has been perpetrated on this poor woman. If she has not yet produced multiple personalities to cope with the problems, she probably never will. It was, however, hard to disregard aspects of dissociation in her behavior, especially in the way she kept staring into space.

I can't handle too many more of these cases, he thought. He was feeling so tired. I will need help from the Guides. Would she, also, be at risk of taking her life? Could one bloody well blame her, if she was?

"Emenohwait," said a well-known voice.

"I'm sick of hearing that word," he mumbled softly, "for Christ's sake."

"So be it," came the immediate reply.

Spirit Guardians are quick to respond and their answers are always appropriate. That's if you get an answer at all. Then you still need to know what they're on about.

Fearful she might have heard the voice, he turned and looked back at his patient. Remarkably, the woman was smiling at him. I should know better, he reminded himself. They flaming well never hear a thing. Relax. But since the Spirit Guardians were likely to be involved, there was little doubt about her being suicidal. So far, the three patients who had come to the clinic when that strange word was uttered had been afflicted in that way. And each of these patients had been in St. Clare's Hospital, where they had met up with the new doctor on their first day. All three had been massively sedated at the time. She might tell me if she knows the doctor, he thought hopefully.

Once again, his mind addressed the Spirit Guardians. I can't handle too much more of this, he told them. My God, it rips my soul apart. This is a job for psychiatry. I'm not adequately trained to take on this kind of a disaster. Too bloody sensitive, I am.

He had to slow his racing mind, and soon. No one could fake the kind of thing she was telling him, ever. This lass is simply not bright enough. Would you call this white slavery? Carnal knowledge? And the rest. . . you'd need to be a lawyer to figure out what to name all these offenses. Bastardry might have to do. Some bitch of a mother-in-law!

The jug boiled much too soon. He brought back the topped-up coffees and was surprised to see the woman could actually spare him another smile.

"Leonie, I have no name for the things they're doing to you," he suggested as he handed her the drink. "Hard to tell. It's complex. But bastardry might come close."

"Just don't say I'm privileged," she replied. Strangely, she now looked utterly composed.

"People don't get the answers to their specific problems by consulting their domestic appliances," one of George's colleagues once told him in jest. "Our refrigerators run too cold, our heaters run too hot, and our vacuum cleaners . . . well, they suck. To do any good in our line of work, George, you need to be a live one. You need cool reasoning *and* you need warm emotions. Therein lies the problem. You must monitor your own behavior and thinking, at least accurately enough for you to know when too much is rubbing off on you. You must know when you yourself have potentially become at risk." There was no need for guessing what Anthony meant.

The two had lost a colleague in somewhat doubtful circumstances.

Anthony was Barnard's friend. He was a contributor and had been a contributor for many years. Months later, he was killed in a road smash that should never have happened. Damn it! He left a wife and four bright little "pups," as he referred to his two-of-each-kind. For many days after the funeral, George remained convinced that for these kinds of disasters to occur—to even be possible—this planet would surely need to be the rubbish dump of the local universe. Experiential life stank, Barnard thought.

Then he remembered to monitor his thinking.

15

"I'm Not Privileged"

Deeply disturbed individuals like Leonie were best dealt with at night. Freed from a tight daytime schedule, he could spend more time with them if they needed it. He could take a break if either he or his patient needed to settle down. Barnard wondered if Leonie knew he organized his work in that way.

Why had she arrived on his first night off in weeks? Why at this unusual time—ten minutes past seven?

"Bundle up your kiddies and get out of there, Leonie," he suggested. "No one on this primitive, empathy-forsaken planet would blame you if you did. Make yourself scarce, girl. I'll help you plan every last move and watch you disappear into thin air."

"I can't! You have to hear it all," she insisted. "You *have* to hear it and you *must* believe me. Nobody does, and I need that. Someone's got to know. *Got* to listen."

"I'm hearing you. Honest, I am."

"I've planned for months and months to come and see you. I checked all the roads on the map, over and over, so I wouldn't get lost. I'm supposed to be in the bowling alley tonight, knocking the pins down and building some muscles. See?" She put down her cup and carefully extracted a piece of paper from her purse. She held it up for him to see. It was a bowling alley score-sheet. "See?"

As he reached out to take it from her, noting her name was quite illegible, he heard her urgent warning, "Gentle with that! It has to stay crisp." Momentarily, her eyes lit up. On her face was an elusive, childlike grin. "Last month's score sheet, but today's date." Her eyes urgently sought for his opinion about this clever trick. That opinion had to be etched on his face, George was sure. "I leave at six-thirty, back by a little after nine."

"Bloody hell. You're near enough a prisoner. Leonie? Child?"

"Yes, and not a very clever one. Not altogether lame-brained either, I am. But not smart enough to get lost in a crowd with my kids and stay lost. And I won't leave them. Never! Never do what my father did to me," she said. Grim determination showed on her face, "and I teach my kiddies what is right. You *must* hear it all."

Shocked into silence, Barnard nodded and vaguely gestured for her to go on.

"They're rich, George. They own more real estate and stuff than anybody knows—and I mean anybody—and they belong to a secret society. They've got friends in business all over the world and they've got friends in organized crime all over, too." She shook her head, a reflection of her thoughts. "Uh-uh. The children and I would be safe in Timbuktu for two, three days, and then they'd find us, and I'd be dead, and that would be good for me, but the children would be lost. Future criminals."

Her misty eyes once more focused on that point in space, but she was still shaking her head. "No, no. It's not safe to shoot through. They're rich and ruthless and mean. And I go to parties with them sometimes, and anybody who is somebody is there. And anybody who is less than a nobody is there with them, as well. Spend any amount on the most expensive gear and make me look a million dollars."

She was still shaking her head, sadly, angrily. "They get half drunk and I get raped by both of them. One rapes and hurts me, and the other one looks on and laughs. They're monsters that own me. . . You have to believe me."

She had stunned the therapist with her life's story. "If there is such a place, Leonie, I will have some dear friends of mine reserve two places in hell for them." It was all Barnard could offer her.

Her response was immediate, "Make that three!" She turned to look him in the eyes as if suddenly awakened. "Make that three, George. She knows what's going on, always did. She always did." With a sad, emotion-filled smile and a sigh, she added, "She's worse. She gets the hottest spot, closest to the fire."

He wondered why she hated the woman so much. Finally, his seemingly frozen brain appeared to thaw a little to give him the needed spark. You feel betrayed, he thought. Betrayed by one of your kind, for she never took the place of the mother who always still loved you. Wake up, George Barnard! Such a bloody big help you are.

"If you won't leave for the children's sake, Leonie, what can I do for you? Cripes! If you just let me, I'll figure it all out and come up with a foolproof plan. There's always a way to get lost and stay lost."

"There's nothing!" she interrupted. "Nothing, George. You have a wife and children, and they're beautiful. I'm well informed. You have business interests, too.

Don't fool with my family; they're dangerous. I only ask that you listen, no more."

"I have a mind designed to solve problems, and I have friends who are infinitely more intelligent than I am. Spirit Guardians." He had said it. And in the fraction of a second it took for her to quickly turn her head away, he sensed she knew a lot more than she was letting on. This desperate woman had indeed met up with a Guardian.

She turned back. "There's nothing!" She momentarily looked like she was about to leave, then thought better of it. "Stuffed into a two-hundred-liter oil drum with lots of cement, and tipped off a trawler over the edge of the continental shelf, your mind won't help you and your Spirit Helpers won't find you," she declared without blinking or flinching. It sounded almost like a threat.

"Jesus! Are they guilty of such crimes?" he asked.

"Knowing about it and laughing about the dead people is just as bad," she claimed. "I hear them talking. They're dangerous! If you listen to me, that helps me. If you understand me, that helps me. If you believe me, that's much better. Because I don't know anymore. Everybody who knows us knows my mother went all funny. They tell people that I act funny, too. They're clever and mean, and I've got no hope. Even our pop-another-pill doctor is in with that secret, cliquey crowd." She bit her lip, then seemed to remember something—something remotely funny, judging by her smile.

"They use you and hurt you on purpose, and if you scream, they hurt you a whole lot more. I learned that quick smart. Clamp your teeth together and shut up if you don't want to hurt a whole lot more. Look at this!" She poked her tongue at him, but in a blink it was gone and she burst out laughing till her tears flowed again.

"I'm not. . . I'm not sticking my tongue out at you, honest," she assured him. "Look at the holes in it. I'll let you see it up close." She walked over to him, still smiling, and she cautiously poked out her tongue again. It was full of deep cuts.

"The one thing I can't stand is a knocked-about, second-hand old tongue," Barnard joked. "Where did you find it? And how much were you charged for it?"

"It's mine! The original," she answered with a laugh. "But sometimes when they hit me, I forget about it and I bite it. I don't know why those little flaps don't heal. They bleed for days." She seated herself again, but much closer to him now. She sighed and quickly checked her diamond-encrusted wristwatch. "Jeepers!"

"You said it, Leonie."

"You have to hear it all, George." Her speech had become more urgent, more pressing. "I'm supposedly rich and privileged and lucky. And I should be thankful. That's what I hear all day long. That's the latest. But I don't know anymore. What have I got? I'm not rich. I'm poor! I've got nothing, only the children. I don't even have . . . me!" She cried softly into a handful of her tissues, then brightened up a little.

She became increasingly more restless as her tale of slavery unfolded and all the pieces of that horrific puzzle of bruises, broken bones, and a wired-up jaw fell into place for her therapist.

At times, her angry voice might well be heard inside the Barnards' homestead. Frequently, her whispering barely touched his hearing range. Now and then, she smiled at him; more often she sobbed. Occasionally, she laughed, though she cried much more readily. Ever more frequently, also, her swollen eyes checked for the precise time on her watch, as if his clinic's timepiece could not be trusted. Finally, she took some money from her purse and placed it on his desk.

"I know how much it is and I can't risk a receipt," she told him. "I mustn't be late."

He watched her stuff the tissues back into her purse and met her at the door.

"You believe me, don't you, George? I *know* you do!"

"You bet yer pink booties, Lady."

"You understand?" she asked.

"You love your kiddies. You won't leave. I understand, Leonie." He briefly touched her on the shoulder and let her hear it loud and clear. "Eh! Girl! I understand!"

"I know now." She grabbed him by the arm like a frightened child. Her lips had started to quiver all over again. "I must never believe I'm privileged, must I?"

"But you are privileged. And you must believe that! But only in the sense that you are the most grown-up lady I've ever met, you are also the most privileged. You are the toughest, the straightest—and in your special, faithful way—the most beautiful person I know."

"Thank you," she answered softly.

"So? Why did I just call you the toughest and the straightest?" he asked.

"I . . . don't . . . know."

"You survived all the physical abuse, but you're too straight to handle the psychological warfare. All that rubbish about being rich and lucky. It's a lie!"

"Oh." She smiled briefly as her mind finally touched on the reality of what he had told her. Then, in slow motion, her face contorted itself to reflect the many years of terror and abuse that had come her way.

"I had to tell you it all . . . somebody. . ." she sobbed.

She swayed a little and seemed unsteady on her feet. Her eyes looked queer, glazed over they seemed. She was about to faint. Quickly he reached out to her. At that very moment, he shared all her deep-felt grief.

⌒

She scurried down the concrete path without looking back. The light of the waning moon guided her to a late-model V8, parked a long way from his door. She gunned the engine into life and drove off at high speed. A long way down the road, the car's lights finally came on.

"I wasn't meant to read your car's numberplate, was I, girl?" he mumbled. "And your name was never Leonie. But I heard your voice, woman. You touched my soul like no other, and I *must* believe you."

He kicked the clinic door shut and flopped down on the settee she had just vacated. He was angry, seething inside. "What's the need for wandering around with a dirty great spear if you're not going to use it?" he bluntly questioned the Spirit Warrior. "Stick those two animals with it, and that useless mother-in-law while you're about it. I bloody well would."

Barnard didn't feel like consulting the Guardians. He only felt like telling them off. "You brought her here! I'm sure you Guys did. You sort her out! All I could give her was a little bit of understanding. Good God! She didn't ask for much."

But he knew she got from him precisely what she came for.

⌒

I penned down your words, word for word, "Leonie." All of this world will know of your courage and strength. Bless you, woman. You will always have that special place in my heart.

For you did nothing wrong.

16

Big John Latimer

None of the patients referred by the doctor operating at St. Clare's Hospital knew the physician's name. None of them had brought George Barnard the customary referral note—not even a business card—and all had inexplicably waited quite some time before contacting the hypnotherapist.

There was an unusual pattern emerging here. The majority of them openly admitted to having a history of attempted suicide. George had to drag the admission out of only a few. All of them were of the opinion that both the therapist and the doctor knew each other well. The man was in fact praising Barnard's work. There was an ever-more urgent need for George Mathieu to talk with him and tell the man to cool it.

Professional etiquette demanded that the treating physician at least send a letter of referral, preferably a full history when it came to attempted self-murder. Ideally, the report to be studied should arrive well in advance of the patient. This practitioner with the Spanish accent was breaking the unwritten rules and leaving Barnard totally in the dark. George could not handle too many more of these special cases.

There was no law stopping him from giving these victims his time. But he felt he had neither the preferred qualifications nor the required experience to do the job well. The sheer weight of their numbers was now getting him down. George Mathieu had always been a rather emotional animal. He would therefore never dream of becoming a full-time therapist.

Barnard was now developing a rapidly worsening nervous rash.

⌒

He easily stood six feet four inches tall in his riding boots, and there was a faint smell of diesel fuel about him. Barnard offered him his hand and watched it disappear into a veritable shovel of a paw—the right kind of equipment for a trucker.

"I've got only one patient to see today," Barnard suggested, "a Mrs. S." He offered the big man a chair, but he was visibly peeved by this man's unexpected arrival. "I don't think you fit her description, John. You said your name was John?" he joked. "Just to be sure."

The big man smiled and nervously touched his Akubra hat. He wasn't about to sit down, but walked off to the far window and looked out. "You might have to burn that tall, dead grass out there," he commented. "I know about those things. I was brought up on a farm."

"Do you think you might get to the point in this present lifetime?" Barnard asked. "And might you have been so fortunate as to have inherited a surname? Please, John, sit down. I'm really pushed for time."

"Yeah, my name is Latimer," the man answered. "John Latimer." He finally took the chair and needed to do something with his big, restless hands. He half unzipped his windbreaker, changed his mind, and zipped it back up again. He was on edge.

"Well, John Latimer, let me warn you," the therapist told him, poker faced. "The woman, our Mrs. S., would be two-thirds your height, and just a third of your weight, if that. But when she gets here in twenty minutes from now . . . sees you sitting in her chair . . . she'll be ten times angrier than you've ever been. I give you fair warning. You've got my undivided attention until then. After that, you're on your own. And no one on this hobby farm with its tall, dead grass can guarantee you sanctuary."

Latimer let out a nervous laugh. "You're just like Allan said you were," he suggested. "I've been hearing about you for years."

"Allan who?"

"Allan Corrighan. Old Hot Rod Corrighan himself. That hairy-all-over trucker. Cough mix, remember? He drives one of my trucks now. He'd pass them all doing a hundred and fifty in a baby's pram, if you asked him nicely."

The man's surname had been enough to quickly bring Allan Corrighan to mind. Four years of addiction to a potent cough syrup—some seven-hundred-plus liters of it over the period—and Allan Corrighan had casually driven his last load right up to the doors of an institute for the mentally ill. That was excellent insight considering the state he was in. Remarkable judgment, really. Two years later, they released him and he was back on the road, still dodging pink kangaroos the size of a barn. But then, he and George had done some good work, kept at it until Allan was fine. Corrighan and the therapist would always be friends.

"How is Allan, John? He and his dear wife? Did he send you? And have you, too, perhaps acquired a liking for that excellent beverage?" Barnard asked tongue in cheek.

"No, not me, never! And they're both okay. No, the doctor told me to go see you and I plum forgot until Allan said your name again. That's when it hit me like a load of slippery bush rocks off a tipper truck. The Doc told me to see you and I forgot."

"Was it Dr. Jasper? Dr. Ian Jasper?" George asked.

"No, the other fellow," Latimer answered.

"Dr. Hugh Byrnes. Did he hand you a note to give me?" George asked. "He always does."

"No, that's not him. The pleasant fellow in St. Clare's. You know him."

There was a sinking feeling in Barnard's stomach, and without conscious thought, he checked the rash on his left arm. He had to find out who this doctor was. The man was beginning to run his life for him. Jeez! I always thought that was my prerogative, Barnard thought.

"I only work with two doctors, John," George explained. "And of those two, only Dr. Jasper is a visiting specialist at St. Clare's. Next to his own general practice work, gynecology is his area of expertise. Now, I'm prepared to give you long odds that you didn't recently give birth, or even fake it. Or that you have something typically feminine wrong with you. You're not the type. Since I don't know any other doctors at St. Clare's, you had better give me his name."

"I don't remember," Latimer answered. It looked like he was thinking hard, touching his forehead and pursing his lips. "He knows you really well, George. Speaks highly of you. Strange I should forget all about the man. And you! Until Allan reminded me."

"You had better describe him to me," Barnard suggested.

"That's easy," he answered immediately, "I'm good at remembering people."

"Give it your best shot, John," George encouraged him.

"Well, he's just average height, slim, about five foot eleven. He's got a healthy suntan, short black hair, and a mustache. Kind of squarish. A brown suit, dark brown shoes, and tie. He always wears a white coat, with the buttons undone, a doctor's coat. Oh, yes. And his stethoscope is always around his neck. That's him. That's the man."

Barnard had heard it all before and in great detail. "He never does up his white coat?" George asked.

"No."

"So? How many times did he come to see you, John?"

Latimer looked befuddled. "Come to think of it, just the once. Just on that one day."

"John, let me see if I've got this straight now," Barnard proposed, "and this might help both you and me. That doctor never does his coat up, his stethoscope always hangs around his neck, but he saw you only the one time. That was the first day, just after you were trucked into St. Clare's, and after you tried to do yourself in. Am I right?"

Latimer looked embarrassed. "I *was* going to tell you, truly," he said.

"I know you were, Johnno," George agreed. "First day in St. Clare's for you. On the drip, perhaps, but zonked out of your skull on tranquilizers, no doubt. Then, here comes the famous Dr. Bloggs and tells you to make an appointment to see me?"

John Latimer seemed to be thinking hard, but he had no ready answers. It all seemed like some weird conspiracy, thought Barnard, with the doctor using hypnosis on all those patients. Was he a doctor? He could be any kind of fool going through the wards, or could he? No! If he was that damn good at it, George felt he could move into his clinic, permanently, and the therapist would take a long break and go fishing.

"Did you tell the man we have a mutual friend in Allan Corrighan?" George asked.

"He seemed to know that already, George," the big trucker answered.

"Good grief!" That answer almost flattened Barnard. "Did he say so?"

"I can't rightly say he said anything," Latimer suggested, "but I know he's got what sounds like a Spanish accent."

"Unmistakably Spanish?" George asked. "Not Portuguese or Italian, Greek maybe?"

"Spain or South America somewhere," the patient assured him. "You can't mistake *that* accent."

~

Mrs. S. (for Simmons) arrived all too soon, but only just a little early for her session. It was fun to see some two hundred pounds of big-rig cowboy alight from her chair like a freshly filled helium balloon. Wow! Didn't he ever get up in a hurry! Latimer had taken George's warning seriously about Mrs. S. being aggressive. The therapist had only been fooling, making conversation to settle him down.

"Remember to burn that dead grass before the rains come," Latimer reminded him once more. Then he left.

"Stacks of spare time. Stacks! Heaps," Barnard grumbled cynically. "Nothing else to do."

With Latimer booked in for the following week, Mrs. Simmons's second-to-last visit out of the way, and just a half hour to spare before he needed to hightail it to his factory, he set about tracking down the rogue doctor. Once he found him, he would give the man a gentle but concise piece of his hotheaded European mind. Coffee in hand, he dialed Dr. Ian Jasper's office.

"Your patient must have given you a bum steer," Ian Jasper—the Barnards' family doctor of many years, as well as a valued associate—stated with certainty. "If the man worked at St. Clare's, I'd know him, George. If he worked in the baby production shop, I'd be holding hands with him," the doctor suggested in jest.

Talking to Dr. Jasper was always worth the time it took. He was good for a laugh.

"If that deviant tendency gets to be chronic," George advised him, "come see me, Ian."

Ian Jasper was brilliant at his work. The patients he referred to Barnard were always the appropriate cases for treatment with hypnosis. They all respected the doctor. It was obvious. Few would realize how deeply depressed their "god of modern medicine" could become when something serious but unavoidable went wrong. Knowledge, intuition, and emotion, wrapped up in one hardworking man doing his long hours, often turned on him with a vengeance. He would then reach for another flagon of port wine. Sometimes he would ring George Barnard to help him drink it.

Two glasses of the fortified red and Jasper turned

into a stand-up comic, four made him sound like the
president of a skeptics' club, six made him a brilliant
philosopher. By eight glasses, he became noisy about his
feelings and often shed a tear. By twelve or fifteen, he
generally passed out.

George hated fortified wines. But he would not
be home until well after midnight, up to the eyeballs in
caffeine.

But one couldn't help liking that medical man.

Dr. Hugh Byrnes was in surgery and could not
come to the telephone. His nurse relayed his message.
There was no practitioner of Spanish origin in the area. If
there was, they would know, and it was nearly impossible for them to get accreditation in Australia. He might be
a herbalist, chiropractor, or some natural medicine kind
of healer.

Barnard was on a wild goose chase, it seemed. But
what about the stethoscope around this man's neck?

The hospital receptionist came back on the line.
"Mr. Barnard, there is no Spanish or South American doctor on our hospital staff. And we have no visiting specialists from either of those parts of the world. That's
checking up on two years, and that's all reception keeps.
Maybe a new intern. That could be. I'll put you through
to Casualty, shall I?"

"Yes, please and thank you."

"I'm only new," came the voice of a young female.
She sounded very new, Barnard thought—no older than
sixteen or seventeen at the most. "But I will go and ask
Lydia. She has been here a long time, ten years, and she
knows everybody."

"That would be kind of you," he told her.

She was back in a flash. "Lydia says no, Mr. Barnard.

But I can switch you through to Administration. I can do that from here." She added proudly, "I do *that* very well."

She sounded cute. Given time, she would do everything very well, with her charming attitude.

"Thanks so much," he told her. "Go for it, girl!"

"These computer records go back eighteen years," George was told, "and they're perfect. But, no. No regulars or specialists from either place. Besides, we would know. No interns either. Of course, we've got some patients with Spanish names. . ." The administrator was only thinking out loud. "It's a mystery, that one."

"I've got it written down here, twice," Barnard commented.

"I can't question that," the man answered. "You've got both Mr. Latimer's admission and discharge dates right. I even remember that big man. He wouldn't fit in any of our beds on that floor. But he will need to give you the name of his attending physician. I can tell you, however, he does not have a black mustache and no black hair—truthfully, not much hair at all now." A kind of sneaky smile shone through with his voice. George could almost see it.

"Thank you for trying," he told the man. "Please don't let John Latimer's legacy wreck a good night's sleep. I'll find his doctor."

There was a chuckle on the other end of the line. "Sorry we couldn't help."

The Medical Association would never give George a moment of their time. It would be against their policy for security reasons. But he might as a last resort dowse for the doctor's name over the open pages of the telephone book. He reached for the yellow pages. "Oh doctor, dear doctor. . ." he wondered out loud. "Wherefore art thou, dear doctor?"

"*Not in your timeframe,*" came the sudden reply. It seemed to resonate throughout the clinic.

It shocked Barnard. "Damn! You scared a year's worth of growth out of me!" he complained.

~

To hear voices when there is no one else around is generally considered to be mentally unhygienic. Talking about it will soon have you branded a crackpot. When engaged in the mental health industry, owning up to your witnessing the phenomenon can be deadly. It must have been during a moment of extraordinary weakness when he confided in Veronah Miller. She was not impressed.

This no-nonsense Lithuanian-born psychologist ran her busy practice no more than a few kilometers from Barnard's home and clinic. She often preferred the use of rather time-consuming hypnotherapy because of the lasting results it produced. She was good at it. Her distinctive accent would have played its part in heightening that success. Veronah and George belonged to the same hypnosis association, and they often sought each other's opinions on various methods, frequently exchanging specific visualization therapies. But telling her about Spirit Guardians and disembodied voices had been a mistake.

"Give yourself some credit," she advised him, "because you are doing a good job. You are showing wonderful results. You have a mind! Why must you invent all these voices to account for the outside-the-square solutions you dream up?"

There was no convincing Veronah that Spirit Guides actually exist.

"What bothers me," she complained, "is that you must invent all these different creatures and different realities of time to house them in. It's all too complex. Life is simple, George. Why make such a mental maze out of it all? For goodness sake, you have a mind. Respect its capacity, instead of hanging on to childhood invisible-play-mate fixations."

He tried once more to convince her of the reality of Spirit Guardians. Like Louise Hewitt, Veronah Miller had at one time been a student of Professor Willis and she respected him. But Veronah saw Willis as a capable psychology lecturer, nothing more.

"The mind is the ultimate last dimension, George," Veronah stated.

"You're right," he told her, "and the Milky Way is painted on the ceiling." He was giving up on her. Deep down, he suspected, his convictions frightened her. She did not want to know, or hear, about the voices.

He would always appreciate those most elusive but audible "childhood-playmate fixations." They were his closest Friends. Their sudden voices, however, often still gave him a shock.

17

Doctor Mendoza

Antoine Julien Barnard was George's older brother. The younger boy looked up to him. After all, Antoine was fifteen years old and tall for his age. As well, he already spoke four languages, read books in another two or three, and had a good grasp of what was going on in the political world.

He also knew precisely how darned smart he was.

At seven years of age, George Mathieu respected him and admired him. He did not always like Antoine very much. This was one of those times. Antoine was standing over him, telling the boy in French how stupid he was. He enjoyed doing that. George hated it.

"For you, George Mathieu Barnard, the fateful day of your life was at the beginning. We went out to purchase a brain for you and we could find nothing but sawdust. That is all. Wet sawdust. That is what one can find between your big ears. Breathe on my face now, and I will tell you if I can smell wet sawdust."

"Leave this young one alone!" said his mama in her ancient Dutch dialect.

"You are again harassing the little man," said Papa in French.

"Nothing can harm wet sawdust," was Antoine's reply. He turned back to his little brother. "It is all English in that book, you fool. It says, a saber-toothed tiger, not a saber-tooth-head tiger." It is a tiger with teeth like a saber, not a saber tiger with a head like a tooth."

"I know it already!" the child told him angrily. "I didn't say it good enough."

"It is *all* you know, George Mathieu," said Antoine. "You are a colossal disgrace to this family. When visitors come, you should be hidden from view. Upstairs. In that dark cupboard would be the best."

"Antoine, you must stop harassing the little man," said Papa. "He is no older than seven, not one-half of your age."

"Yes," said Mama, "leave this young one be. He shall learn *so* well."

"I will know everything," George told Antoine.

Antoine burst out laughing. "Everything?" he asked.

"*Everything!*" George shouted at him. He was convinced he would.

"For you, George Mathieu, upon this excellent news, we will prepare some fresh sawdust, immediately," Antoine promised the boy. "Then I will look forward to the day you tell me something I do not already know. After that, we celebrate. All day we celebrate. All night we celebrate." He laughed and returned to his room to learn more things from his books, saying, "A saber-tooth-head tiger. What a curious animal. *Mon Dieu!* How totally unique!"

"Can sawdust be put in people's heads?" George asked his Papa. He wanted to be certain.

Theodore fleetingly looked up from his newspaper, frowned at the boy, and said, "*Non.*" Moments later, he again glanced at his son. "If you want to know everything, George Mathieu," he suggested, "you will need to live forever."

"I can do that," the boy assured his papa.

"We searched around the shops for many days," said his Mama, "and spent all our money to pay for the best brain we could find."

George knew that would be right. She always took her time when shopping, and she went for the very best quality when she finally made up her mind. One day, his expensive brain would know everything, and he would tell Antoine something he did not already know.

That would fix him good and proper.

～)

"Not in your timeframe." It was still ringing in George's ears.

"Thank you for the information," he mumbled at the owner of the voice. "I could have been told a long time ago." He thought some more about what he had just said. "I jolly well could have been asked first," he complained. "It is a matter of common courtesy. Even on this bad-mannered planet, we still tend to first communicate about what we would like the other person to do. This fact might have escaped your notice," he suggested sarcastically. "Look at the flaming red rash on my arm! Jeez! My nerves are all in a tangle with all these people trying to off themselves. And if this Spanish-sounding character is not associated with us, I don't want any more of his referrals, if you can call them that."

He had stated his case and he would stick by that decision. They all knew he would. If they were not listening, some Seraph would soon get the message across that Barnard wanted no more. Seraphim are incredible gossips.

"The Dutch are stiff-headed enough," he suggested, "and you can never convince a Frenchman of anything. You Guys have got me. The worst of both those races wrapped up in one. No more! Finished!" he told them, but he knew he might perhaps reconsider should someone else turn up.

It is called workaholism, caring, and wanting to know everything, not necessarily in order of importance.

But George was concerned about the identity of the "medical man" who lived outside his timeframe. Fear of the unknown is one of the greatest driving forces known to man. It frequently compels us to do things we should never even contemplate. It often causes us to do sweet nothing when we should act.

He had no idea who that supposed medical man was, where in time he was, if he was associated with Ahbécétutu and Andréa, or simply a ring-in who was muscling in on a well-established work arrangement. "I am human. And I have fears."

The clinic curtains drawn, and the light dimmed, he spread himself out on some pillows and drifted into the realm of the Spirit Guardians. Gently, insistently, he deepened the trance to the frequency of his Next in Command. Minutes went by. This had worked well so far, but nothing was happening yet. Ahbécétutu might be busy, he thought. But so am I.

Finally, the mighty, well-armed genius Sentinel, his sharp eyes still scanning the horizon, effortlessly synchronized with the human timeframe and materialized no more than a few paces away on the screen of his mind.

"I welcome you, Bzutu," George Mathieu greeted the Guide by his nickname, and added with a smile, "I would never take you away from your well-deserved lunch break or siesta if it were not for John Latimer and stacks of other guys who want to leave the planet in a hurry. I need to borrow your great mind." There was no response from the Warrior.

Since it had been made clear to George Mathieu, directly from the mind of this great Spirit Guardian, that "Ahbécétutu never sleeps, eats, ages, or forgets," he presumed all Spirit Guardians to be suffering from the same chronic insomnia and hunger pains, and to have difficulties in coping with the concept of a fading mortal memory. They would also accumulate incredible knowledge and wisdom.

George had also taken note of the fact that the Guide claimed to have always strived to be a contributor, and that his Seraphic Superiors would vouch for him. However, Ahbécétutu was less than impressed with his own endeavors of a distant past, during a time "when there is no Law." It was clear to George that this was circumstantial, hardly the Guardian's fault, although Ahbécétutu wished he had done even better.

His memory being intact, even since ancient times, the Spirit Guide should be able to accurately reflect on all he might have done better. Unlike mortal man, he should more clearly grasp the folly of his ways and more precisely sense the need to do what is right. But it would not be possible for him to look back on these failures to excel, and still retain a semblance of self-worth—Celestial Intrinsic Credit, you might call it—unless a sense of humor and optimism about the future were also distinct aspects of his personality.

Knowledge and wisdom, the time/space existence of which cannot be divorced from learning, experience, and accurate recall, would therefore demand the genius Sentinel to be in possession of a brilliant sense of humor. It would also necessitate his having supreme confidence in the long-term future of his planetary home, as well as his survival as a personality. That's how George Mathieu reasoned in purely human terms. Those terms might not even apply to Spirit Guardians. Who would know from their abrupt, short, or monosyllabic answers? But perhaps he simply hated George's jokes and the mortal was wasting his time. It was rare to see the Warrior smile.

"I was only kidding, Bzutu," George admitted. "But truly, you have been without decent sustenance and sleep for a long time," he tried again. He decided the pun was lost on the Warrior, knowing his mind. "We have business to discuss, my good Friend. This South American rogue of a medical practitioner, or Spanish—whatever he is—is loading me up! Look at my left arm! A trace element or B-group vitamin deficiency, because my nerves are rattled from one day to the next, and I can't take much more of this. What is he?"

"He is One, one, one, one," answered the Guardian's mind as he turned to face the human rookie.

"Is he honest in his ways?" George asked.

"He is all ways vouched for," came the answer.

In all ways, George thought, bar flaming consideration for mortals. "He is pushing me too hard, Bzutu," he complained.

"It is important," was the immediate answer.

"So is my mental health," George fired back. "I have a wife and family, Bzutu, if you hadn't noticed. Other patients, and a dirty great factory full of men and women.

And they've got families, too. Stacks of responsibilities for one mammal."

"It does not last, George Barnard."

It won't last, George thought. He had perceived that mind-to-mind term before. He knew what it meant. The doctor was on temporary assignment. A projected cluster of likely suicides, perhaps. "Neither will I last, my Friend," George answered. "No sooner am I born, and I'm a wrinkly old man compared to you Guys. This will greatly hasten the process."

There seemed to be a glimmer of appreciation for that thought. The Spirit Guide shifted his weight, a sure sign he was contemplating the humorous aspect of what a mere mortal's mind had put to him. But a troubling thought struck Barnard. It felt as if his blood had run cold.

"You're not giving me to him, are you?" George wanted to know urgently. "I don't think I like him very much. I rather belong with you and Andréa and Simone and Juliette."

"We are one," came the answer.

It was clear their platoon was not to be split up. George gave a sigh of relief, suddenly realizing how much he would miss them all if they were to part company. Although the Spirit Guardians had been elusive until quite recently, the group had been together for a long time. George would likely refuse to work with anyone else, especially someone like this new Guy. He had no manners, Barnard thought.

"The Doctor belongs to another platoon?" George questioned almost casually, certain the answer would confirm that the new Guide had muscled in. But the response was negative. This new Fellow did belong to their platoon. And instantly, the mortal realized they might well be a far-flung organization. They weren't just a cozy bunch of freaky, local freelancers.

"What's the Doctor's name then, Bzutu?" he asked. "I need to know. I always need to know whom I am dealing with. It leaves me with a marginal sense of independence, and that makes me happy," George suggested.

There was a look on Ahbécétutu's face that said, "Don't I know it!" A jumble of letters appeared on the screen of the mortal's mind, together with the now well-known sound, "Emenohwait." That made sense!

How come he hadn't gotten it before? It seemed so obvious now. Emenohwait was MNO-8. And the ancient warrior Ahbécétutu was ABC-22. Later, it would be revealed that Danielle's friend, Simone, was MNO-6.

"How marvelous!" George grunted. "You are doing it again, Bzutu!" he complained. "I do not want his tax-file number or his social security code. That might be his car's number plate or the digits on his credit card," he laughed. "Give us the good doctor's name, for heaven's sake."

Less than a second elapsed and George sensed static. A high-speed information blurb, directed upwards, was coming from a Spirit Guide to the Warrior's right. That was probably Andréa at work, perhaps the Seraph, Juliette, but George could not see anyone there. It was all too fast for his slow-moving forebrain to decipher. The upward-directed signal elicited an instantaneous downward-directed response of a similar kind—undoubtedly it was a request for approval of some kind going up, and an explicit positive response coming down. That was all his mind could gather at the time. It came so fast!

Instantly, it arrived in picture form on the screen of his mind—a section of whitewashed stone-built home, on the corner of a street, far away. More than ten feet from the ground, attached to the wall, was an aged street sign. Some of its weathered blue paint had flaked off.

George strained his eyes to make it out, "Via . . . MEN-DOZ-A? MENDOZA! Dr. Mendoza!" he concluded. "Fine! Thank you! Thank you all." He was ever so pleased. He laughed at the Sentinel and joked in mock sarcasm, "Gosh! What took you so long?"

There was a mere illusion of a smile on Bzutu's face. The Spirit Guide, knowing the fickle responses of this human subordinate so well, was not offended, just vaguely amused. There was, however, the feeling that he needed to soon depart. The occasion was rare when their contact had lasted more than a few minutes. This surely was one of them.

"Give us a quick look at him then, if you must go," George pleaded.

An image of the Spirit Doctor, like a hologram, arrived in an instant, and Barnard checked it out. John Latimer, he concluded, sure had an eye for detail, even when tranquilized out of his skull. In seconds, the image was gone and his attention was once more drawn to the Warrior's eyes.

"Latimer, Bzutu," he reminded the Guardian, as if he needed reminding. "You Guys brought that easygoing fellow to my clinic, but he's a waste of time, because he won't reoffend, will he now?"

Then, as the other likely outcome of Big John's short stay on the planet was projected, goose bumps appeared all over George's body. He shuddered. This was the first time he learned of the potential finality of suicide. It churned his stomach around. "I'll fight, Bzutu, for all of us. We fight. We win. We all ways win."

There was no show of emotion from the Warrior. High-speed communication ensued. It was too fast to comprehend, too accurate to either distrust or dismiss. It would surface in Barnard's mind, effortlessly, whilst he treated Latimer. He knew it would. It always did. And Latimer would be fine.

The Guardian needed to depart. Soon, he and his razor-sharp shimmering spear would fade and disappear. But George Mathieu wanted more. "We are comrades and Warriors, you and I, Bzutu," he reminded the Spirit, with a poker face. Bzutu might give me half a chance if he stops reading my mind, he thought. "Were we both red, were we both black, or both of us white—shock, horror—we could be even closer friends."

With baited breath, he waited for Ahbécétutu's reaction to his racist fooling around, but there was no response from his Superior.

"I was only kidding, Bzutu," George admitted, "but I can see you know this already. And I don't care what color you are. You know we will always be friends, as we've been for a long, long time." He laughed at the Spirit Guardian, "We are as old as the hills, you and I."

"You are older," came the clearly audible and startling reply. Ahbécétutu was acknowledging the presence of George's Spirit Self, first and foremost!

"Jeez! You know something? That is what has crossed my mind . . . I think . . . many times . . . Wow! I've got all these vague memories of other lives. . ." Barnard paused to think about what the Guardian had said. "Gosh!" he added, "I had better start acting my age."

"What takes you so long?" Ahbécétutu asked. Then he was gone.

⌒

The activities of Emenohwait the Healer, or Dr. Mendoza, as George prefers to call him, since even the therapist's pet goldfish have proper names, soon came to an end. Mendoza's duties at the local hospital, St. Clare's, lasted only about six months, perhaps a little longer.

The fallout of the Guardian's activities, a veritable stream of "attempteds" coming to Barnard's clinic, left the therapist in a state of emotional exhaustion. Not until Dr. Mendoza's tour of duty was almost at an end did George finally get serious about finding out who the Doctor was. And when George did get to see him, it likely was the brilliant minds of Ahbécétutu and Andréa that showed him only the image of the Spirit Guardian, via a moving, three-dimensional, full-color thought transference.

They can do that so well.

18

Jacyntha

Having nothing to do for an hour but wait near the railway station of the big city, George Mathieu found himself a seat under some shady palms. It was only eight o'clock and already the tropical sun had a sting in it. He watched the people walking by. People without smiles, without pleasure in their lives, without a word to say to another. The workforce of the big city—hardly awake, pressed for time, hassled, humorless.

People, people, people. Gray people . . . wearing their masks.

She was quite beautiful. But no! To George's eyes, she was ravishing! Blonde, quite tall, she wore high heels to make herself look even taller. She had on a short black skirt. Phew! Very, very short. She would have been eighteen at the most and she walked towards him pushing a stroller, slowly, almost seductively, with an air that said, "I'm so proud of my baby."

Almost in front of him, the strap of her shoe slipped from her heel and she stopped, and their eyes met only for a moment in time. Without bending forward, she lifted her leg high and pushed the strap back, without any risk of exposing her well-shaped behind. What a clever, well-practiced move!

Of course, Barnard only had eyes for the sleeping infant and, excitedly, he said to its charming young mother, "Doesn't he look just like his father!"

"Do you think so, too?" Her response had been immediate. Then a frown and a smile appeared on her face. "Oooh," she made. "You wouldn't know!"

With a smile, the irrepressible trickster held her sparkling eyes on his face, but he would not say another word.

Some ten minutes later, he spotted her again, on the opposite side of the wide road and at some distance. That obstinate strap had slipped once more, and she was fixing it in her skillful manner. She turned and smiled at him across the way. Then she spontaneously waved him goodbye, before moving on with her precious little charge.

Having nothing to do for an hour, he waited under the palms. Away from the sting of the tropical sun, he watched the people walking by. People without smiles, without pleasure in their lives, without a word to say to another. The workforce of the big city—hardly awake, pressed for time, hassled, humorless. People, people, people. Gray people . . . wearing those masks.

And he wondered when the young mother would lose that glow, that sparkle in her eyes, that carefree honesty, that clearly observable awareness of her intrinsic values, that sense of humor, to put on a dull gray mask like so many others wore.

And he prayed she never would.

"We are both bloody idiots!" shouted a man some distance away. George knew the voice and recognized the accent. It belonged to a friend, an engineer and businessman who had arrived in the country knowing little of the language. But he had picked it up quickly on the motor vehicle assembly lines of his adopted country. His Hungarian accent would never change, nor would his boisterous behavior. It had been well established by the time he was hurling Molotov Cocktails at invading Russian tanks. Zoltan Kovac was striding towards him.

"Bloody daylight savings," Zoltan laughed as he shook Barnard's hand, "and we both forgot about it. We do not like it in this state. It fades the premier's curtains two times as fast, and his cows are unhappy. They turn on the milk taps one hour too late. How the hell are you? You must go to our beach house, put salt water on your arm, and do nothing," he suggested.

It was good to see his Hungarian friend again after quite some years. He looked healthy and prosperous. Kovac had landed a huge engineering contract and he had sounded excited about it over the telephone. But George had asked him for a temporary job, any job.

"I've got to have something to do," Barnard pleaded with him. "You know I can't sit still. I need to be on the go to help me think."

Zoltan ignored him completely. "I remembered about daylight savings this morning," he said, "and I am thinking, what will George do for an hour? Sit under the palms! And there you are." He paused to formulate a cautious question. "You want a job for one week? All the planning is done! All the brainwork is done! Only the manufacture of these transmitters. Put them all together and you have six kilometers of the bloody things. A stupid job. Not for you. The planning is done . . . you want a job for one week?"

"Give me a stupid job for one week, Zoltan," George repeated. "My brains are numb."

"Give up this hypnosis, George," he suggested with a laugh. "This psychology lessons crap. Hop in the car now. . ." Kovac skillfully edged into the traffic. "Hypnosis! Shrinking brains! I would be good at that! 'What is your name? Write it down. What is your problem? Good! Write it down. Now! Pull up your bloody socks and go about your business. Do not come back, you stupid idiot!'"

Both of them laughed about that blunt statement. George knew that Zoltan meant every word of it. He would never suffer from a severe nervous breakdown, Barnard mused. He isn't the type. At the time, neither of them would have believed that within that year, Zoltan would crash from his exuberant, dizzy heights to an all-time low. He would make the long trip to Barnard's home and clinic, stay with the family for a week, learn more about emotion than he ever thought existed, and slowly pull himself up again by the bootstraps—a much wiser man.

But as they trundled down the street in Zoltan's car, George thought, no one could ever down this wild Hungarian.

He was so wrong.

"You would absolutely thrive on repeat business, Zoltan," George suggested. "Patients would come flocking to your door by the hundreds for a taste of your extraordinary bedside manner."

He ignored George's comment. "You want a stupid job?" he asked again.

"A week of routine work in a new environment will stop me losing the plot, Zoltan. That's not an unusual prescription," the therapist answered. "I need a short break away from everything to decide if I'm going to go for that machine parts project that's in the offing. But I can't be away for too long, or I'll miss more than a few important psychology lectures."

Zoltan was thinking about it long and hard. Finally, he suggested, "Okay. You can work with the Eurasian girl, Kimmie. She's really good. She lost her teammate and she's struggling by herself. She's my best little casual worker, and I feel really bad about her not being able to get going. They're bloody heavy things, and you will have grease and paint and crap all over you."

"The dirtier the better," Barnard suggested happily. "I'll thrive."

"You could go to our beach house and do nothing," came the suggestion once again. "Plenty of beer in that refrigerator for six weeks."

The thought of having his former co-director of some fifteen years past working on his factory floor somehow embarrassed Zoltan, it seemed.

"Working hard and not thinking will be good for you?" he finally asked.

"Sometimes, if prescribed," George told him.

"Prescribe yourself my beach house and cold beer," he said and laughed. "Get your second opinion from Doctor Zoltan Kovac!"

That "stupid" assembly job was indeed a two-man task. In their case, one man, one Kimmie Wong. She was a descendant of the old Chinese gold miners of long ago with a fair bit of European thrown in. She was earning herself some extra cash to pay for her all-important nursing studies and was ever so pleased she was no longer alone at the job. With the loss of her teammate, her output had instantly nosedived, and she now felt utterly obliged to catch up on the losses of two previous days. It suited Barnard. By that Thursday afternoon, her face was aglow with pride and exhaustion. They had not only caught up, they were heading all but one team.

"Tomorrow we'll be the furthest ahead," she predicted.

"You can stake your great-great-great-grandfather's gold mine on that bet, Kim," George promised her.

"I'll be sorry when you go," she remarked.

"Zoltan promised me you'll have a new teammate on Monday," he told her. "He's ever so proud of you."

She seemed very happy with his comment. Her eyes lit up. "Are you his friend?" she asked.

"Not really for all that long. Just for the last two hundred years, Kim."

"Are you an engineer?" she asked.

He shook his head. "I have a factory down south where we make a few things. But I actually get paid for asking questions in one of my jobs," he joked. "Do you?"

She had missed the pun. "I'm curious. Why are you here?" she asked.

"Just for a break. To stop me from going right up the wall." Answering people's dumb questions! he was thinking, but he didn't have the heart to say it.

She seemed to need some time to absorb the information. There was something on her mind, George was sure. She wanted to tell him something and did not have the courage. "Will you come to a housewarming party with me?" she suddenly asked. "Tonight?"

He needed to give her request some thought. That wasn't it, he was sure. She is trying to extend the amount of time we will be together. She wants to know me better before off-loading some deep-felt problem.

"They're all med school students," Kim added. "They're all working to pay for their education, just like me. They're a well-behaved crowd, if you should wonder. . ."

It was approaching ten o'clock, and still the food kept coming. Their Chinese hosts were excellent cooks and the banquet they put on was delicious. One of the two was in Australia just to study a particular form of acupuncture with electrical impulses. It surprised Barnard, who might have traveled to China if he wanted to learn about that.

For the third time that evening, he reassured one of the young Oriental guests that he did not own a philosopher's stone, and if the fellow thought George's aura was telling him he did, he needed to check his books on the subject. He was reading something else in the aura. But George wasn't prepared to tell him his mind was "adjusted" to communicate with the 11:11 Spirit Guardians of the Halfway Realm.

Suddenly a young woman burst onto the scene. She was dressed in smart business attire, hardly your typical gate-crasher. She was in her early to mid-thirties, tall and slim, but in a dreadful state of mind, and looked very ill. It was difficult for anyone in the group to understand what she was shouting about, but slowly it became clear to them all. Her thirteen-year-old daughter had died the previous day from a massive overdose of drugs. The impetuous teenager had talked too much, the mother said.

The child had been done away with.

This young woman was now all alone. Divorced from her husband at a very young age, she had managed to look after her only child by herself. Now that she had lost her, she was left with nothing in the world. No one to love or be loved by. No one to care for. The sorrow was driving her out of her mind.

She was on a mission to find a man called Frank. She believed Frank had intentionally given her daughter the overdose.

She was losing the plot, and rapidly. She loudly accused all those present of harboring Frank. Then she accused all of the men, individually, of being Frank—all of them except George Mathieu. And perhaps the therapist might have seemed to be a little too old to be Frank, even to her befuddled, desperate mind. Then she accused everyone collectively of being Frank. That's when the therapist became very concerned about her. She was raving and ranting and pushing her metabolism higher by the minute, deeper into insanity.

Suddenly, in his mind, Barnard saw the home of Frank. It was only five or six doors down the street and on the same side. She would surely not live much longer if she managed to flush out the drug dealer. She might end up on an urgent mission to join her daughter. The very next moment, she was saying just that. This ashen-faced female was going to be with her thirteen-year-old—her punishment for a crime she did not commit. The crime of losing an impulsive, reckless youngster. Barnard had to do something, and quickly. He needed to go to her and, with a high-speed induction, turn her hysteria into controlled hypnosis, settle her down, let her see the senselessness of another wasted life. But he could not move!

He was stuck to his seat and looked around for someone to help him get out of the chair, or for someone —anyone—one of the psychology students, to delay the young woman while he battled with the gravity of a dozen Earths. Then his mind told him to calm down and wait. Her anger had to run its course. He remembered the Maria Morgan healing. He was being controlled. It was happening again.

In amazement, he looked around at the other guests. All of them to grow up and become healers? No one in the party—four of them psychology students, two of them to go on to year three—seemed to know what to do for this sad, bereaved young woman. They were sitting there, stock-still, flabbergasted, but perhaps they were stuck, just like he was. Again, the woman confirmed his fears that she was soon to die to be with her girl. She was raising her voice, more and more. Then she stopped to take a deep breath. The tirade of seconds ago had become a deadly silence. But there was more coming.

"Listen to me!" Barnard told this tormented young woman. His voice was harsh. "Listen to the words of an old man who has also been pulled through the wringer of life!" The violent epileptic fit that almost cost him his life, and the severe beating that was the cause of his condition, was again so clear in his memory.

Again, his mind told him to cross the floor and touch her on the forehead. He knew it was all that was needed for her to be healed, but he was locked in his chair by a Force he did not know. Catching up with the echo of his voice, he was to belatedly comprehend the words he had already spoken, and that never came from his mind. "You will not find Frank in this room. All the people here are healers, each in their own way. All of them are contributors. And you, also, have got this great amount of energy . . . so negative now, but it can be turned to positive use. You must go and fight Frank by working in drug rehabilitation. Not by finding him and losing your life as well."

It was the Spirit that had spoken, was still speaking. He could no longer listen. He was whisked away from this place. His get-you-there-at-the-speed-of-thought Spirit Self was doing all the work. It had happened again. This young woman was getting the instructions for what was to become the rest of her life, directly from the Eternal Documents of the Future.

He was back in the room at last. The woman was going around shaking hands with the guests, hugging them and kissing them, saying, "I am Jacyntha. I am so sorry for what I said. I am so pleased I met you all. I love you so very much. I love you all. I know what I must do." There was the Golden Glow all around her. She looked so healthy.

One of the guests, an osteopathy student seated next to Barnard, turned to him and said, "George, that was *beautiful,* what you just told this poor lady."

Trancelike, he turned to her and frowned. He was not too sure he had said anything at all. He sure remembered he was going to. What had he told her? Hours after, it began to come back to him. Days later, snippets were still surfacing, but in this life, he may never recall it all. Much time has passed since that day.

Jacyntha was ready for battle. Like a storm trooper

with a mission, she marched out of there. Suddenly, George realized he was drenched. Soaked in perspiration he was, and little Kimmie Wong supported him all the way as he stumbled back to his flat.

Exhausted he was, from sitting in his chair and letting Someone Else do the talking.

"That knocked all the stuffing out of you," Kim said as she pushed him into his chair.

"How did you do that, George?"

"I don't really know," he answered. "I must have felt really sorry for the lass." It was still not clear to him what had happened.

"Wish I could do that," she said. She was pouring two coffees.

"You can learn," Barnard suggested. "For me there seems to be no escape from it anymore. Wherever I hide. And, to be truthful, that's what I thought I was running away from. But if you really want it, then go for it, Kim."

She turned on her heel and said, "No! I spoiled my chances!"

He would have guessed Kimmie's age to be about twenty-five. She was thirty-four. That was a surprise to him. She was sipping her coffee, sitting close by on the rug and looking away from him. Her back was bent, her shoulders hunched.

She needed to talk.

He had felt this discussion coming on since early that afternoon. She was obviously still in two minds, but he gave her the space.

"I wandered around Asia for four years," she began. "Thailand, Bangladesh, India, Pakistan . . . I can turn up almost anywhere, slip into the local drag and look like a native of the place, behave like one too. I was searching for . . . I don't know what. It ended up being heroin. That's what I found." She glanced up at him, monitoring his expression. "You never even batted an eyelid, George!" It sounded like a complaint.

"I've heard things like that before," Barnard answered.

"Are you a psychiatrist?" she asked.

"A clinical hypnotherapist, Kim."

"That explains it," she replied.

"Fill me in, won't you, Miss Wong?"

"I would never tell anybody what I've done," she replied. "I've come right across the continent from the cultured-pearl town in the west, Broome. Even changed my name. And then you walked in. And I knew I was going to tell you everything I've done, and you wouldn't tell a soul. I knew that. You would never even tell Zoltan, and he's your friend."

He smiled at her. "I've got this chronic hearing disability," he suggested, "and you are very sharp, Wonggie. You picked it right."

"I was so spaced out on heroin most times," she carried on, "I wouldn't know what country I was in. Waking up occasionally and looking at my passport to see who put a stamp on it last. I've had sex with so many men and I can't remember any of their faces. Can't remember what it felt like. Can't remember where I picked up what venereal disease. Always more men interested in me. Always more money. Always more heroin into my veins."

"I'm listening, Kimmie," he assured her as she looked up once more to see if he was paying attention to her life's story.

She carried on, "I don't even know how I got back to Western Australia. I must have saved a heap of money and gone without fixes, or stolen it. I don't know. I shook off the heroin with methadone, and the methadone with a lot of screaming, yelling, and vomiting. I got all the bugs flushed out of my system and lost my ovaries in the process. Got a job, made some cash, changed my name, and disappeared to the East Coast. Here I am. Kimmie Wong. Good choice of name, eh? Talking to a fellow I won't see again after tomorrow. What do you think about that?"

"I'd love to have that name for myself," he suggested. "I'd look the part."

"About the crappy life I gave myself! And telling you, George!"

"Oh, that. How do you feel about it?" he asked. "That's what matters."

She looked him in the eye and said, "I . . . feel . . . so . . . good. Kind of healed."

"Yeah, I can see that. You really needed to let go of all that crap."

"Why?" she asked. "I was determined not to ever tell anyone."

"Something had to catch up with you, Kim," Barnard answered.

"Why tell you?" she asked. "I know you're leaving on Sunday, but I wouldn't be nervous about it if you were around until next month, or next year."

"That's your intuition," he answered. "Pat yourself on the back for getting that right. But you left the heroin behind, the methadone, the transmitted bugs, even your name—your ovaries, for that matter. But you forgot to let your self-esteem catch up with you, to build it up, girl. That should have been packed into your suitcase first." He waited until she looked up at him and queried why he had stopped. "Kim, a part of you is still wandering around Thailand—wherever—playing the arch-slut of the century. That was then. This . . . is now."

She was catching on; he could tell by her eyelids squeezing ever so slightly. "Yeah. . ." she whispered. She needed to think some more, realize what she now was.

"You've worked your little butt off for Zoltan, making up for lost production that was never your loss. Your workmate left. Zoltan's bad luck and he knew it, and he was truly concerned about you battling it out on your own. He knew. You did not. So, where was your self-evaluation, your self-esteem, in taking all the responsibility for your not doing enough? Think, woman!"

There was a big smile blossoming on her face. It stayed there.

"How are your marks at med college, Kim?" he asked.

"The best," she answered. "College is a breeze. Shooting up with that filth never even affected my brain. I got lucky. I've seen some guys . . . oh, God. . . Don't even think about it."

"Whom do you tell about your good marks?" he asked.

"There's no one to tell!" she answered. "I shot through! I left no trail!"

"There is someone," he insisted.

"I wish there was," she sighed.

"There's you, Kim. Tell yourself how good

you are now, and nothing can stop you. You have not spoiled your chances."

Although neither of them said so, they were both talking about her chances in an afterlife.

Slowly, her back straightened itself, her shoulders moved back. "We're still going to beat all the other teams tomorrow, eh?" she asked.

"We will!"

"Are you going to start that machine parts undertaking when you're back with your family, George?"

"Yes. I've decided I'm totally fearless after all," he joked.

I Question...

Why this morning's unseasonable dusty whirlwind
    had to blow away my freshly sown radish seeds.

Why, only yesterday, a lightning strike out of the blue
    targeted the tallest and most beautiful tree in our
    park to scatter its splintered trunk
    right across our children's playing field.

Why, just the other day, that beautiful orange-tailed
    black cockatoo had to have its wing amputated
    to save its life when it will never fly again.

But I certainly must know why, scarcely a week ago,
    that young mother had to die in childbirth,
    leaving the innocent babe the hunger of a lifetime
    for her mother's love.

I question the purpose of all this wanton pain
    and destruction
    and this makes me a rebel.

What can we learn from this
    when we can seldom make it better?
The task is awesome, too great.
Where to begin?
And when is payback time?

part seven

Payback Time

As the managing director of his little company, George Mathieu Barnard made all the
important decisions. If Kevin Weiss had not been
aware of this fact in the past, he certainly knew
now. Despite the production manager's litany of
complaints about the machine parts project, the
long-term contract was now signed. Production
had commenced.

As a therapist, a professional problem solver,
George's decisions were limited to what kind of
advice he would give or what kind of therapy he
would employ. Only his patients could decide
how to live their lives, solve their problems, and
conquer their shortcomings.

In his role as a parent, Barnard had of necessity taken many backward steps. Jodi ran their
strict, somewhat regimented household almost
entirely by herself. To the children, Barnard represented bedtime stories and fun to be had, dumb
stunts and things to be learned, rowdy games to be
played, and even plain, delightful chaos.

In his continuing studies, Barnard knew
what was required. There was research to be
done before a certain date. There were essays to
be written of three thousand words and not a

stray syllable more. One did as one was told, precisely—or else.

But in his relationship with the Spirit Guardians, the psychic's obligations as well as pre-rogatives, rights, and freedom to act were far from clear. There was no how-to handbook for Mortals in Association with the Spirit Guardians of the Halfway Realm, no advertising brochure, not even a leaflet that George Mathieu could obtain on the matter.

He was about to learn how important he was to the Guides.

Shortly after, he would find out about the lowliness of his rank in the platoon.

19

The Fire

"What would you like for Christmas, Sean?" Barnard asked the fire captain of their local Bush Fire Brigade at their annual get-together.

"Five inches of rain," was the spontaneous answer, "coming down slowly, between Christmas Eve and Boxing Day. But preferably three weeks sooner, like right now. She's going to be a bad'un, this year, George" he added.

Five months of drought, cloudless skies, and scorching sun was rapidly taking its toll. There had been no spring, it seemed. Trees were dying, creeks were dry, and grass was brittle and complaining underfoot. Many of the regularly seen birds had simply left the district for better accommodation elsewhere. Lots of marsupials had been forced from their forest homes. They were visiting farms and people's backyards, now outwardly unafraid of man.

The kangaroos had stripped every leaf from Jodi Barnard's treasured rose bushes. El Niño was still on the march and had given itself a flying, early start for the new season.

"I stepped outside my door this morning," Sean carried on with a deadpan voice, "and what do you know. Here's this six-foot lump of a kangaroo buck, already waiting for me. At six-thirty, mind you."

"Came to check if your fire engine was in working order?" Barnard suggested with a laugh.

"No. He asked me for a drink of water. I told him, 'You've got to be kidding! We're out of water too, but you're welcome to a cold beer.' So, he went and got all his mates for a booze-up."

Sean Patchett was serious about life, but only when there was a fire.

Fires were Sean's enemy, to be ruthlessly targeted by him and his small army of volunteers.

"Your ten hectares of that tall, dry grass really is a trap, George," he admitted. "I drove onto your land this morning, before you were up. And as you said, it does provide a corridor between that scrubland and the State Forest. One spark of lightning anywhere around there, or a kid with matches in the scrub, and there's nothing to stop a fire for miles and miles. Your dwelling is at risk, as well. Your clinic even more so."

"Shall I get someone to slash it for us?" Barnard asked.

Patchett shook his head. He looked like he had scarcely heard George's question. "That grass is too dry, too old. We'll back-burn," he finally suggested thoughtfully. "It'll cause an ugly mess, but it'll look good when the rains finally come. Saturday? Late in the afternoon?" he asked.

"Fine with me, Sean," George told him.

"I'll bring a crew. You can give us a hand if you wear the right gear for the job."

It was the least Barnard could do to help with the burn-off. Weeks of working long hours on the new machine parts project had left him fatigued. But he could hardly be absent when others worked on his little hobby farm.

⌒

Sean had parked his big red machine well beyond the field, under some trees and away from the likely stream of ashes that would soon be raining down. George was surprised by the makeup of Sean Patchett's crew of seven as they climbed down from their fire truck. All of them were barely teenagers, both girls and boys. One of the girls looked to be no older than nine or ten. All of them were the children of Sean's regular volunteers. But each was decked out in neatly fitting bright yellow coveralls, wide headgear, masks around their necks, feet planted in sturdy boots. All had large drink bottles.

How well organized!

It was an aspect of Sean's abilities Barnard had never stopped to consider. The man sure had a way with the youngsters. They looked like a cute, miniature version of a real brigade as they lined up neat and straight to receive their instructions.

This was to be a controlled burn-off, they were told. A path one meter wide would be burned along the State Forest fence. The same would follow all along the land of Barnards' neighbors, the Walters. Weeks ago, the main road had been fireproofed, but the private road, home, and clinic would need much scrutiny when the main fire was lit.

Armed with black wattle branches and dripping-wet potato bags, Sean's platoon was ready and eager to do battle.

"Where's Frankie Walters, George?" Patchett asked.

"Still on vacation, up north."

"Uh. Darn," the fire captain said. "Unfortunate. We might burn a tuft of his grass, and this community will see the beginning of a protracted civil war."

They both knew he was joking. Frank Walters was easygoing. It would have been reassuring, however, to have Frank and his family standing by.

"Put your drink bottles in the water trough!" Sean addressed his crew with an air of decisiveness. "Get ready, the six-and-a-half of you," he ordered, with a big smile at the baby of the team. "You let it burn until I say, 'Go!' Then you can hit it for all you're worth. Rotate around, like I showed you before. We all get our turn at it."

He lit the fire. "Let it burn . . . let it burn, Pattie . . . let it burn. Go! Hit it on the head! Good girl!" Slowly, the fire crept along the State Forest fence, with scarcely a breeze to push it ahead.

"Let it burn . . . let it burn . . . let it burn, Richie. Now! Let her have it!" One could feel the children's excitement. "Let it burn, Joel. Hit it! Good boy!"

This has to be Sean Patchett's very own trained circus, Barnard mused, as he watched the excited children. They were plying their wattle branches the moment he gave them the go-ahead. Those waiting for their turn were hopping up and down in the ashes, laughing and chatting. It was the junior brigade's very first real job, and they loved every minute of it. Soon the entire field was made safe by a neat trail of gray and black ashes.

"Where do we light it, Uncle Sean?" one of the young ladies asked.

"Put your finger in your mouth," Patchett told her. He watched her do it. "Right. Now stick it in the air like this. What do you feel, Sandy?" he asked.

"A wet finger!" she answered, frowning at her captain.

"Give me patience," the man grumbled. "Which side got the coldest, girl?"

"The outside, for sure!" she answered. "Not the inside." She had a mischievous look on her face. "The side of Mr. Walters's land," she added quickly. "Is that where the breeze is coming from?"

"Protect us all, I ask you, Lord, from the ladies that descend on us innocent country folk from the Big Smog," Patchett grunted, his face lifted to the heavens in mock prayer. "Yes, from the south-southwest."

"So, where do we light it then?" she insisted.

"It hardly matters where we light it, Sandy," he told her. "There's nearly no breeze. But right here is the correct spot, if we're going to be fussed about it. Come on, you rascals!" he shouted at a little troop that had strayed to jump around in the ashes. "Now comes the easy bit, and all you need to do is watch it. Line up behind Mr. Barnard and me and fan out as the fire grows. If, and only if, there are spot fires outside our safety trail, or on the other side of Mr. Barnard's driveway, you can hop to it and put them out."

Excitement and anticipation glowed on their faces. They were ready for action, clearly wishing for spot fires to jump the trail. They would descend on them like vultures and obliterate the fires.

"Here she goes!" Sean Patchett lit the grass, and soon pale blue smoke columned into the clear, late afternoon's summer sky as the fire took hold on the bone-dry grass. Everyone spread out along the perimeter of the field. Wattle branches and potato bags in hand, they were all ready to pounce on spot fires and cinders beyond the well-marked boundaries of the field.

High up and almost touching the sparse clouds, the big pillar of smoke abruptly changed course to rapidly sweep to the south. There's a mighty powerful breeze up there, George thought. Sean Patchett had also noticed it and was watching it with a look of disbelief on his face. Barnard walked up to him and asked, "Did you ever see that before, Sean?"

"Oh, yes," he answered, "but not at this time of day, and not too often at this time of year. Strange. There are no isobars across the entire state, and not a breath of wind down here. Up there, it's going the wrong way at a rate of knots. It's got to be a local disturbance. The weather report said sultry, no wind."

Relax, relax, relax, George told himself. Give it an hour of this. Think of the emerald carpet you'll be seeing when the rains come. But he felt uneasy for not having consulted with the Spirit Guardians.

A sudden gust of wind from the north flared the hungry flames many meters into the air, then the wind dropped again as quickly as it had picked up.

A small fire crackled sedately behind the barbed sheep wire fence of the Walters's property, and in an instant George leaped over the obstruction, easily quelling the flames with his boots. A second gust from the north hit him with a wave of piping-hot air. He noticed two more spot fires as he squinted his eyes to look through the distorting, seemingly liquid air. A moment's indecision, then he ran to the perimeter to quickly stomp out the farther of the two. He doubled back to the center of the field to do battle with the second of the fires. It had grown to be quite a task.

"You picked the trickiest weather in years, George Mathieu Barnard," he heard himself say. "Never bothered to check with the Spirit Guides, you loner."

Quickly he checked on Sean and the children. They were fine. All of them were busy putting out spot fires with the rhythmic lashing of their wattle branches and potato bags as a wind squall struck from the east. This one would put the homestead and clinic in danger should the fire jump the break. Only one of Sean's crew was stationed there. She looked so tiny and forlorn. She would be frightened, George thought. He ran along the fence to join her.

"Put it all out!" Sean Patchett bellowed to his crew. "The whole damned lot!"

They had all heard his baritone voice over the crackling and the sizzling of the fire. Steadily, doggedly determined, the entire Patchett team closed in on the monster blaze, but each time it appeared to be beaten and tamed, a fresh gust of wind angered it again.

Each time the wind-driven, hungry tongues of flame devouring the dry grassland forced the band of little firefighters to retreat, they bravely regrouped to again drive back their common foe. Twice George saw Sean Patchett sprint away for the distant fire tanker, and twice he was forced to return as the beast of a fire threatened his charges.

"We shall win this battle for our home," Barnard grunted at the exhausted little one who was fighting by his side. Her cheeks crimson, her mouth open, she had long ago taken off her smoke mask. Perspiration was gushing from her face, but she was still smiling as she pounded her wattle branch on new outbreaks, over and over.

"We will win. We will win," he mumbled as he landed feet first onto another spot fire and kicked some burning branches into the mouth of that fiery demon threatening the family home. We will win, his mind insisted. But we are not winning. We are slowly losing our grip on this fiend.

He was needed on the northern front line, as the breeze turned again. He left the youngster to the task and raced through a clearing in the fire.

Powerful doubts pervaded his soul. We might lose the scrub, the Walters's farm, the forest, the homestead and clinic. That beast of a fire is toying with us all.

They were all exhausted, dehydrated, and overheating in their protective clothing. George felt near to collapse.

Sean Patchett was setting off for another dash to his fire engine, as a sudden wind squall from the south whipped the blaze into a frenzy. Immediately he returned to be with his crew as the youngsters and George all fled from its ravenous path. Immediately, the children regrouped once more to ply their sacks and branches to the fresh spread of fire.

"We are stubborn!" one of them shouted. "We never give in! Come and get us!"

But George had given in. There was no more fight in him. He dropped his wattle branch and momentarily surveyed the carnage. Then he raised his face and arms to the sky and shouted angrily, *"Jesus Christ! We need a change of wind!"*

Motionless and perplexed, he stood there, arms and face raised to the heavens as if sculpted from stone, as a wall of ice-cold air from above and from the north pinned down the flames and instantly extinguished the fire.

Motionless and perplexed, Sean Patchett stood there, no more than twenty paces from Barnard, as if frozen for all time. Only his little troopers retained their presence of mind and jumped with urgency on the last remaining cinders and smoking grass polls.

It took the fire captain many, many long seconds to slowly turn and stare at George in utter disbelief. His hair poking down in tufts from under his helmet, his mouth open, his face flushed and soaked in perspiration, he raised his questioning eyebrows at Barnard.

Finally he managed to say, "He heard you!" Sean was quiet for a long time, looking at the children, absent-mindedly, it appeared. Then he looked back at George and said, "That just doesn't happen." Again he paused. Then he clarified his statement. "George, the wind just don't ever blow up or down like that."

Barnard was still too shocked about the sudden rescue to answer him.

"Come on, all you kids!" Patchett shouted at the troops. "Get your water bottles! Under the trees! And one small sip at a time!"

They were all installed under the trees when George Barnard remembered he owned a pair of legs.

Sean Patchett was a down-to-earth kind of man, a contributor. Much of his time was freely given to the community, and most of his activities concerned the fire truck, the depot, and his teams of volunteers. No one paid him for his services. Sean had simply adopted the entire community. And, although he had always come by to collect the Barnard family's donations, for they were contributing but nonactive members, he never visited their homestead again. George never heard another of Sean's jokes. The Barnard family never received another invitation to the Patchetts' home.

What happened on the day of the grass fire was something Sean Patchett's emotions could not in any way deal with.

Much the pity.

∽

It was dark and quiet in the cellar. It was also the closest refuge to the half-burned field where George's overheated body could slowly cool down. Sean and his energetic tribe of youngsters had left, seemingly none the worse for wear. George was exhausted from the all-out battle, numbed by the instantaneous deliverance from the demon conflagration.

Seated on the cold concrete, leaning against the cold brick wall, he was trying to come to grips with what had happened. Sean would have the customary solution. He would simply shut it out from his day-to-day memory. George could never do that.

"You saved us from the nearest thing to hell. You saved lives, perhaps, and our home, Frankie Walters's farm, the clinic, the scrubland, the forest. . . God! Miles and miles and miles of forest."

"Was this payback time? Who am I, then, that for me You put out the fire?"

"Did I ask You to? Did I beg? Did I plead with You? Did I appeal to You? Did I for once pray to You for You to put out the fire?"

"Indeed I did not. I just about ordered You to put it out. And like a helpful Older Brother, You accommodated a spoiled sibling. I insisted, demanded, and expected to be heard, and You heard my voice, is that not so?"

Outside the window, on a twig of the oleander bush, a tiny, double-barred finch bobbed its head.

"If You say so, I shall have faith. And I promise You this also: I shall not ever again scorch Your Earth."

20

Psychometric Revelations

The Spirit Guardian looked somber, unwilling to communicate, it seemed. For some days
already, there had been difficulties with, first of all,
George's finding them, and second, his extracting
needed information from them. As well, it seemed
only Ahbécétutu was prepared to show up. Both
Andréa, and the Seraph, Juliette, might well be
around, but the mortal was unable to perceive
their presence in any way.

"There's a vacant settee for you here,
Bzutu," George subtly informed the Guardian.
"Stretch out your weary body and be sociable.
Take a break and talk to me."

Bzutu's stance was not that of a happy Spirit
Guide. His eyes conveyed that George should be
feeling shame, embarrassment, even guilt. But the
human was feeling neither shame nor embarrassment. And, long ago, he had lost the need, and
indeed the capacity, to feel any kind of guilt.

"You may not belong to a cult!" came the
loud, spoken reply.

At least here is some response, even if it is a
direct order, Barnard considered.

Warnings were common, suggestions were
few. A direct order was decidedly rare. Here,
also, is an attack on the legitimacy of my franchise
to determine my own actions, he felt.

"So, what have I done?" the mortal questioned. "They are a harmless bunch of Christian

freaks, Bzutu. Marjory, Daryl, and I are only investigating this crowd. We might actually learn something useful."

The Spirit Guardian's bossy attitude was irritating George, and the Warrior would already know this directly from the human's mind.

It seemed not to matter to the Guardian. *"You may not belong to a cult!"*

"I heard you the first time," George mumbled at him under his breath. Ahbécétutu should know I would never dream of joining a cult, he thought.

Not until after he was gone did George realize that something already stashed away in his mind might be at risk. The Spirit Guardians might well be aware of an event in the future that Barnard could not foresee. Something this cult was teaching might be on the nose. But the mighty Warrior's attitude had upset his pig-headed mortal underling.

George and his friends would make one last visit to the headquarters of this unusual cult.

In the "business of psychometrics," Professor Willis was an absolute genius. In one of their training sessions, George's co-student, Louise Hewitt, was able to quickly locate in her mind the previous owner of an ornate brooch that she had picked out from among a number of objects. She described the English lady, Willis's mother, in great detail. Louise had ever so swiftly passed all her tests with flying colors. Lou Lou was also brilliant at psychometry.

When it came to Barnard's turn to psych out an item of jewelry, he saw a beautiful vision of an old jeweler working on the item. Then the craftsman handed the brooch across a workbench to a young lady, a mere child, who set about polishing the jewelry. "We are in Paris," George told Willis. "It's got to be old, this thing. . . This is eighteen hundred and something. God knows. . ."

But the owner of the brooch remained elusive. George, it seemed, wasn't very good at doing this psychometrics stuff.

It had indeed been made in the late eighteen hundreds, Ted Willis confirmed. But he did not know where it was made. Perhaps George Barnard's being a manufacturer had steered his mind towards the manufacture of this item. There was also the French connection. And, then again, perhaps his entire effort had been a dazzling flop. Willis really couldn't say. Was his student bothered about not knowing?

No. Either way, George would not lose any sleep over this possible failure or unusual but misdirected success. Psychometrics didn't interest him one iota. He had no practical use for it. And if it bothered the professor, Willis could always find out for himself.

Someone handed George a basket with all kinds of personal items in it, and he picked out a tiny ring with a violet stone. The vision came almost instantly. Here was a nasty-looking thistle with strong spines, growing in barren soil. And as he watched it, the spines fell off, one by one, until they were all gone. The curly, hairy leaves turned smooth, and a magnificent flower sprouted from its center. There it stood in rich, fertile soil, aiming itself at ample sunshine, with many others of its varied species all around.

"Your new home environment is much more conducive to progress," George told the owner of the small ring. "You are enjoying life now, and have many friends. The past looks miserable, not very beneficial to your advancement or to any project. You needed to be on guard there, constantly defending yourself. Whatever it was you were into, you're very lucky to be out of it now." George sensed that her spouse had possibly mistreated her and that she had recently left him. But he didn't really know and didn't want to say any more.

"How dare you psychoanalyze me in public!" the young woman snapped at him.

"How dare you put that ring in the basket when I'm around," he suggested to her. "I'm doing stacks of psych assessments. It's my infernal job, woman! And what you just got is hardly an analysis."

She thought for a moment. "You're right," she told him. "Old habits die hard. I tend to shoot first and ask questions later. You must forgive me."

"Sure . . . you just lost another of those sharp spines," he said. "You'll be fine." But he wondered what kind of desperation had brought her to this place. What sort of environment was this for a confused young woman? There were some unbelievably nonsensical concepts being promoted by some of the spaced-out members of this unusual cult.

Some were getting the 11:11 courtesy wake-up calls, or so they said. And this was generally translated to mean the world would end on November the eleventh, perhaps this year, perhaps next year, and may-the-Good-Lord-have-pity-on-this-crowd, perhaps at precisely eleven minutes past eleven.

And perhaps not at all, George's ever-sarcastic mind told him.

He had been dearly hoping to meet someone who might also have vocal or visual contact, or both, with the Spirit Guardians of the Halfway Realm. That would make being with this odd conglomeration of people, who were not affiliated with any particular path or group, all worthwhile. They would be able to exchange untold masses of precious information. So far, he had not found anyone who even knew a Spirit Guardian. Ahbécétutu might have wanted to save me from wasting my time, he thought.

It was approaching midnight. Only a few candles were still burning in the center of the big hall. People were constantly tripping over each other, but at least the cult's electricity bill would be manageable. The group, some forty-five members in all, mostly young women, were seated on the floor in a large circle.

Someone was passing on a message from the Archangel Gabriel. Wow! George was smiling, and quietly considered applying for the job of official speechwriter for the exalted Entity in his next life. He would surely get the job, and a hefty wage increase. What a load of dribble was this speech!

Then that dumb basket came around again. Ahbécétutu was right. George was squandering his time in this place, plus two hours of driving there and back.

His lucky dip in the darkness turned out to be a lady's watch.

"What I sees, I says," Barnard told the motley congregation with a laugh. "If you don't like my private video session, I don't want to know about it. And you don't get your money back on this one."

Someone in the crowd was purposefully clearing his throat. George was being irreverent so shortly after Gabriel's departure, it seemed. But the Spirit Guardians' student was bored with the extensive psychometric content of their haphazardly thrown-together "religious" program.

"It's a lady's watch I have here," he told the group. "I'm watching a young woman cleaning her pretty little home. It's white with green trim and dark brown guttering, and she is sweeping out the last of the dust. She's been busy, this girl. The place is now spotless. There is a low wall of bright red bricks, and on it rest two light-blue, fluffy bathroom mats, drying in the sun. I'm looking at her kitchen garden now. It's well laid out and almost completely weeded. The garden faces north, and she has planted everything in rows, but there are no paths between the rows. The smallest vegetables are in the front; the tall, but sturdy, sweet corn is at the back. Everything will get ample light. Nothing will overshadow anything in this garden."

Suddenly, there was a warning. "Whoever owns this watch," George said with some urgency, "you are not meant to take the weeds from amongst the sweet corn. If you do, you'll trample on the rest of your delicious vegetables. That corn will grow tall and broad and suffocate the weeds."

That was the end of the vision. He placed the watch

back in the basket and returned to his place.

"Thank you," said a soft, sweet voice right next to him.

George looked at the young woman and smiled. "Did you get the meaning of it all?" he asked.

"May I speak with you after?" she asked in turn.

He nodded. "I'll see you outside," he said, "but I'm getting out of here soon."

The vision had come in full color, and with it had come the concise meaning. The young woman had swept her boyfriend, partner, or husband completely out of her life. They had parted company, but had since engaged in some heart-to-heart discussions about their differences, judging by the cleanliness of the bathroom mats. The mats were almost dry, and thus reconciliation was practically an accomplished fact. Nothing stood in the way of a renewed permanent, loving relationship. The red brick wall was only low, easy to scale.

She had joined this way-out Christian cult, and the careful weeding of her garden was indicative of her sticking to some basic rules. She had managed to make great moral and spiritual progress. She was, however, intent on her partner also joining the cult.

The warning was clear. If she were to set about weeding the corn—telling her partner how to go about his life—she would quickly damage her healthy-looking vegetables—destroy her own life and happiness. The entire garden was receiving ample light, so there was no reason why their diverse interests should become a sticking point in an otherwise excellent relationship. Her new-found fundamentalist attitude greatly concerned George. This was a vital turning point in the young woman's life. Soon she would either make it, or wreck it for good.

He quietly considered that, had this been an ordinary dream, he would have had no hope of translating it. Somehow—God knows how—all the meanings had come with the multicolored vision. Things were happening in this place, but some of them he didn't like. Next up, they were told good old Moses himself was going to make a speech.

George had had enough of it. That was all he could take of this circus.

The young woman had left just ahead of him and was waiting for him outside the hall.

"What's the big fellow's name?" George asked her.

"Bernie," she answered. "Actually, it's Bernhardt. He's German. He's so set in his ways. You can't tell him anything!" came her bitter complaint.

She had made him laugh. She looked rather cute when exasperated. "You can't ever tell any German anything," he joked, "but I like him. Stop picking on the man! Let the corn grow tall, and let it smother its own weeds. Let him find his way, and in his own good time. He had a most stable upbringing, this fellow. You can't make him join this religion thing, but you can at least admire him for not rubbishing you about your sudden change in direction. Put yourself in his shoes. No! Put yourself in his corn patch."

She looked happy. "He loves his corn, but I don't like it, even though I am the vegetarian. He isn't," she said. "He eats meat, that primitive Neanderthaler." Obviously, she had understood the entire message contained in the vision. Under normal circumstances, it would have only made sense to her, little sense to George. Yet, the meaning had all been there for him.

"Are you a guru?" she suddenly asked. She had a

delightful openness belonging to someone much younger, he felt.

"I've had as many professions as you've had birth-day parties," he told her, "but guru is not yet on my list. I'll work on it and let you know, kiddo."

He needed to make his way home. His patient friends, Daryl and Marjory, were waiting for him in his car. It was late. They would be tired. "I've gotta go," he told her. "Be nice to Bernie. What's your name?"

"Debbie."

"Be nice to the Neanderthal Man, Debbie," he laughed.

"I'm going to visit him tomorrow," she answered, "and ask him to come back."

"Charm him into it," he suggested. "You can do it. You've got what it takes, lady. That irresistible smile of yours will even make a German go weak in the knees. *Jawohl?*"

"Are you coming back?" she asked with a smile.

"Not in this lifetime," he answered. "No way!"

"I don't think I will, either," she told him pensively. She walked some distance towards her car. Then, child-like, she skipped the rest of the way.

You meet all kinds in this life. She was a lovely, cheerful character. Moments later, George faced the most evil "thing" he ever met in this world.

~

He was dressed in all black, and only an hour before, had been spouting the most horrible language. He had been a disciple of a well-known Indian guru, he told all who wanted to hear. Prior to that, he had been a devotee of Satan. Now, there is a guru for you! You might have to be a bit desperate, though.

But with so many weirdos in the place, George had not taken him seriously either, and he soon turned his back on the fellow.

Although all the others had remained inside, this strange man had followed Debbie, Daryl, Marjory, and George into the car park.

During the time Barnard spoke with Bernie's future bride, the man stood at a distance of perhaps forty meters, well out of earshot. Yet, his eyes were on the two at all times, as if he were listening in on the conversation. Stock-still, unblinking, his attention was continuously directed at the two. He was just a faintly unsettling presence to them, no more.

George passed him on the way to his vehicle and raised his arm in a silent greeting to the man. But this fellow did something very strange, and this instantly caught Barnard's eye. The man's mouth fell open, and his head moved to one side until it nearly touched his shoulder.

To George it seemed the fellow was almost certainly triggering a rather powerful alpha brain/mind rhythm. At that very moment, it caused an excruciating pain in Barnard's head. It was all he could do to stagger to his car, grasp at the roof rack, and momentarily hang on for dear life. When George turned to look back just some thirty seconds later, the man had left.

To this day, Barnard has no idea what it was the man did, or how he did it, other than to insist that the man must have surely used an altered state of consciousness to inflict such pain. Neither does he want to know how it was done, nor does he ever want to suffer that again. That was agony! But George wonders what this misguided young fellow could do with that awesome power if he set out to heal people, rather than hurt them.

Daryl drove them all home that evening. George was in great pain at least for an hour after that psychic attack. But Daryl and Marjory could not accept that someone could have caused his discomfort. Caffeine withdrawal or nicotine withdrawal, or both, they suggested to the man still smarting in the back seat of his own car.

In two or three hours? There's no way! George had no doubt whatever about the cause. That young man in black did that strange thing, and, instantly, George was in pain. And Barnard is getting rather weary of hearing that word "coincidence."

Not even George can comprehend what could have motivated the fellow to do that to him. He was a visitor to the place, not even a potential member.

Is it possible that Satan has no temporary employees or disciples? In his insane cult, life membership is probably the only option, Barnard concluded.

Satan should have disclosed that fact on his recruitment forms.

Have I made enemies in "hell"? Good! I'm stoked about that! he thought.

George knew he should have listened to Ahbécétutu and not returned to the cult. But it wasn't just Bernie, the Neanderthal Man, you could not convince of anything. Barnard always had his own stubborn Cro-Magnon streak.

"Got you at last," the mortal told the Spirit Guardian. "This planet swarms with vertebrates of my kind. There's nowhere left for you to hide. I'm obstinate, my Friend. I keep looking and, sooner or later . . . I find you."

"We find you," the Guardian disagreed. He was making it clear that if he didn't want to be found, he would never be.

Ahbécétutu's later mind-to-mind explanation of what happened to George outside the headquarters of that cult made no sense whatever. It left the mortal contemplating that the cause of his inability to understand could only be his own, very human, comparatively abject poverty of conceptual capacity.

The Warrior tried to explain. George knows he did. It got them both nowhere.

"Insubordinate you are," George was told at last.

"I only wanted to know what was going on in there!" he cried.

"We guide you," came the mind-to-mind reply.

"I'm more than a robot! Cripes! I have a mind. Did you not know this?"

Their short meeting broke up with the message, "You are told so many times." It simply meant, "You were duly warned, you fool of a mortal." But Ahbécétutu can put it so kindly, and succinctly.

It had been payback time for his insubordination, and Barnard knew it. But it was still in the early days. The level of their human-celestial communication and cooperation would soon attain a dizzying height of excellence.

But looking back on those tentative first steps, one must truly feel for the Guardians. No sooner have they trained a marginally psychically talented, slow-on-the-uptake dreamer of a mortal to be of some use in their enterprise of planetary progress, than the creature's life comes to an end. Again they must search for another rookie to take that place.

The brilliant minds of the Halfway Realm must at times be subjected to unimaginable frustration in their efforts to impart needed information to the most confused and backward species that dares to stray all over their universes.

Homo sapiens sapiens? Gosh!

What a misnomer!

What of the Earth?
What of Its People?

For every river we pollute,
    one child will be born,
    and he will speak many languages.

For every tract of forest we clear,
    one child will be born,
    and she will carry the blueprint of our future in her mind.

For every species we deplete from our domain,
    one child will be born,
    and he will speak of great things when only a
    babe in arms.

And for every nation we oppress,
    one child will be born,
    with her mind attuned to the urgings of the
    Spirit Guardians.

A new race is now appearing, and in ever greater
    numbers.
They are our beloved children,
    who will save us from ourselves.

The 11:11 Documents

The Search for 11:11 is the first in a series of five books that comprise the *11:11 Documents*. In the forthcoming volumes listed below, George Barnard continues the story of his personal spiritual experiences—and treasured adventures of others who are working in cooperation with the Celestial-Mortal Alliance.

In the Service of 11:11

By the Grace of 11:11

The Winged Eagle: A Healing Journey

The Anatomy of the Halfway Realm: A Spirit Guardians' Student Handbook

CDs containing manuscripts of the above works are available for purchase via the 11:11 website

Next in the Series

In the Service of 11:11

When George's only son is in danger of drowning, it is the time-distant Andréa who, expending enormous personal energy, reaches through from the Midway Realm to the human level. It is the genius-minded Andréa who warns her mortal student of the calamity in the making, showing him what is to happen and telling him of the advanced intelligence that "comes from far in time, far in space." The warning is in fact "Paradise-acknowledged data" forwarded to Andréa. The seemingly inescapable drowning is avoided, and the eternal debt George now owes this androgynous Spirit Guardian cements their friendship forever.

This second book of the 11:11 series, which documents these events and many other exciting experiences of the 11:11 Emergency Platoon, is due for publication in 2004.

11:11 Services

We invite you to visit the 11:11 website at

www.1111spiritguardians.com
www.1111publishers.com

and review the archived transcripts of celestial contact with George and other receivers. You may also provide your e-mail address for inclusion on the 11:11 International Progress List, and you will occasionally be sent transcripts of recorded contact with various Spirit Guides, Angels, and other Celestial Teachers.

Guided meditation/visualization CDs are available to facilitate your spiritual pursuits. CDs containing the other manuscripts in this series being readied for publication are also available for purchase at the site.

Are you one of many favored mortals
who are also receiving 11:11, perhaps 3:33,
or other double-digit time-prompts?
We would like to hear from you.

Please contact us via our website.